The Case for a
New Bretton Woods

The Case For series

Kevin P. Gallagher
Richard Kozul-Wright

———————

The Case for a New Bretton Woods

polity

First published in 2022 by Polity Press

Polity Press
65 Bridge Street
Cambridge CB2 1UR, UK

Polity Press
101 Station Landing
Suite 300
Medford, MA 02155, USA

ISBN-13: 978-1-5095-4653-4
ISBN-13: 978-1-5095-4654-1 (pb)

A catalogue record for this book is available from the British Library.

Library of Congress Control Number: 2021942106

Typeset in 11 on 15pt Sabon by
Cheshire Typesetting Ltd, Cuddington, Cheshire
Printed and bound in Great Britain by TJ Books Ltd, Padstow, Cornwall

For further information on Polity, visit our website:
politybooks.com

Contents

1

The Fierce Urgency of Now: The Case for a New Bretton Woods Moment

We are now faced with the fact that tomorrow is today. We are confronted with the fierce urgency of now. In this unfolding conundrum of life and history, there "is" such a thing as being too late. This is no time for apathy or complacency. This is a time for vigorous and positive action.

Martin Luther King, 1967

At the height of the Vietnam War, Martin Luther King called for vigorous action, on both the domestic and international fronts, to fight injustice and prevent the world heading toward "violent co-annihilation." Today, such action is just as urgent to tackle polarizing inequality, growing economic insecurity, and a breakdown of the climate system. While the policy responses must be linked to local needs and experiences and will require dedicated and determined actions by national governments, the

1

increasingly intertwined nature of these challenges can only be effectively tackled with the support of ambitious global action and coordination.

Promoting international cooperation is, to a large extent, the job of the multilateral system that emerged after World War Two. The question is whether that system is up to the scale and urgency of these challenges.

Multilateral institutions have no doubt contributed to the unprecedented levels of aggregate income enjoyed in some parts of the world and to the documented falls in extreme poverty in others. But over the last three decades they have drifted a long way from the intentions of the 1944 United Nations Monetary and Financial Conference to strengthen the ability of nation states to meet progressive social and economic goals through a balanced system of international rules and actions that would mitigate the risk of mutually destructive economic behavior, foster cooperation for shared purposes, and guarantee sufficient space for governments to tailor policies to local circumstances (Ikenberry 2020). That conference, held at Bretton Woods, New Hampshire, was not some cozy diplomatic conclave content to agree a set of goals and targets that promised a better world. Rather, its ambition and outcomes reflected profound shifts in political thinking and hard-fought power struggles, in particular between what Harry Dexter White, head of the United States delegation, dubbed the "coming" (the United States) and "going" (the United Kingdom) nations (Kuttner, 2018).

But international power struggles are not just contested among national governments. As we note in the next chapter, after World War One financial interests and central bankers were quick to recover the reins of economic policy-making and advance their interests in the incipient multilateral arena. The result was an international economic regime tuned to the demands and wishes of footloose capital, ready and willing to employ austerity measures to fulfill them, and far too relaxed about the sharp rise in inequality, insecurity, and indebtedness this implied. These economic forces not only played a role in subverting the League of Nations' fledgling efforts at international coordination as economic tensions began to mount toward the end of the 1920s, they also helped fuel the rise of right-wing populism, authoritarianism, depression, and, ultimately, war.

The international economic order imagined at Bretton Woods was designed to preclude a return to the chaos and despair of the 1930s. Its shape and practice would depend, critically, on how the United

States employed its recently cemented hegemonic status. New political coalitions had brought Franklin D. Roosevelt to power in the 1932 election and put employment, economic security, and social justice at the center of the polis (Schlesinger 1958). Even as World War Two was still raging, the Roosevelt administration was intent on doing the same at the international level. The key to success, according to Henry Morgenthau, Roosevelt's Secretary of the Treasury, and host of the Bretton Woods conference, was to drive "the usurious money lenders from the temple of international finance" and make capital serve "the general welfare" (Morgenthau 1944, 121). Morgenthau was unduly optimistic. Financial interests would soon push back against Roosevelt's New Deal, opening up economic and legislative cracks and crevices both at home and in the international system. From the 1980s onwards they would assert ever greater influence over governments (and people) across the world.

Almost eighty years since Bretton Woods, the world we live in bears an uncomfortable resemblance to the one its delegates hoped would be gone forever. This has not been caused by right-wing populists such as Donald Trump, but by powerful interests who have rigged the rules of the economic game to maintain a winner-takes-all world of privileged individuals and corporations, in which the institutions of multilateral governance designed to foster responsible sovereignty and underpin social stability have instead curtailed the policy space available to governments and preached economic austerity (Mazower 2013: 421).

The operation (and breakdown) of that same system has, moreover, accelerated the climate crisis by undercutting the possibility of large-scale public investment, spreading feelings of political neglect, and deepening the sense of anxiety on which right-wing populists, who see climate change as a hoax, have fed. The global financial crisis of 2008–9 and the Covid-19 health and economic crises have exposed the fragilities of this system. The international community has, on both occasions, failed to respond appropriately.

This book makes the case for a fundamental resetting of the Bretton Woods institutions. By that we do not mean convening a three-week summit to tinker with the rules and treaties that govern international finance, trade, investment, and intellectual property. Nor, however, do we mean a wholesale abandoning of those institutions. Rather, building back better will require a renewal of public institutions and collective goals at the national level, along with new principles of international cooperation and global leadership, that together can rebalance the relationship between capital, labor, and the natural environment in a way that turns "prosperity for all" from prime-time sloganeering into the *senso comune* (common sense) of international economic cooperation.

The Takeaways from Bretton Woods 1.0

Efforts to reconcile the requirements of national governments with their international entanglements have a long history (Mazower 2013). What made Bretton Woods distinct from previous multilateral initiatives was a recognition that combining national economic goals with international peace and stability would require dedicated public institutions to ensure "the fullest and most effective use of the world's resources." The architects of these new institutions had to contend with three abiding and closely related challenges of global governance. First, how many resources and policy responsibilities could they procure from sovereign states to manage a supportive international environment (the sovereignty challenge)? Second, how would international policy priorities be set and responsibilities established across a diverse membership (the leadership challenge)? Third, how, if at all, would those who benefited the most from international cooperation compensate those who benefited the least (the distribution challenge)?

As will be further elaborated in the following chapters, there are four main takeaways from Bretton Woods that, we believe, remain relevant when thinking about governance in relation to contemporary global challenges:

1) *Face up to failure.* Austerity does not work; the gold standard and the outsized influence of financial interests had triggered widespread depression, insecurity, and conflict. A new order would require an ideological break with laissez-faire and adjustment through austerity.

2) *Treat markets as means not ends.* Economic security, personal safety, social justice, energy choices, and political representation should not be left to the dictates of markets. Prices and property rights can help to achieve more inclusive growth and development but require complementary institutions, effective regulation, and shared values that the market doesn't itself provide.

3) *Forge a set of shared national goals and common global interests.* The international order was

constructed to support the national goals of full employment and social welfare by providing five key global public goods: a stable monetary and exchange rate system; a global lender of last resort to provide liquidity to distressed nations; counter-cyclical and long-term lending; open markets' including under recession; and a coordinated international economic policy.

4) *Nurture cooperation.* Rather than ad hoc summitry and bilateral policy negotiations, a set of permanent institutions is needed to monitor, coordinate, and guide the interdependent economic system into the future.

These ideas underpinned the creation of the International Monetary Fund (IMF), the International Bank for Reconstruction and Development (IBRD), the General Agreement on Tariffs and Trade (GATT), and their subsequent extensions and offspring. While far from perfect, this was a powerful attempt to globalize economic relations while maintaining sufficient policy autonomy for nation states to pursue a broad set of economic and social goals.

In this book we make the case that a spirit similar to that of Bretton Woods needs to be evoked if the twenty-first-century global economy is to become more stable, more equitable, and environmentally sustainable. At the same time, the practice of multilateralism must change profoundly to meet these objectives, and with respect not only to its recent neoliberal deviation, but also to the original post-war multilateral model which relied unduly on American hegemony and was never able to properly accommodate development goals.

From Managing Capitalism to Enabling Capital

Financial interests were noticeable by their absence from the Bretton Woods conference. That was no accident. Disciplining the behavior of finance capital was seen, by the architects of the conference, as key to the stability of the post-war system. But those interests resented the constraints on their activities and were quick to push back and sow seeds of discontent in the years immediately following the conference. New coalitions were established to finance political parties, candidates, and an apparatus of experts that pushed for a revival of classical liberalism, first in national capitals and then at the international institutions themselves (Blyth 2002; Gallagher 2015). The overarching philosophy is now referred to as "neoliberalism," which pushes for unregulated markets and individual freedoms as primary ends, arguing that "free trade," "free enterprise," and the unbridled movement of capital are the only guarantees of a healthy economy and widespread prosperity.

These efforts achieved some early success, but not enough to reverse the ideological tide in support of social solidarity and interventionism that had emerged from the wartime experience and continued to animate policy discussions over the following three decades. They began to yield more bountiful returns from the early 1980s with the abandonment in advanced countries of full employment, the privatization of state-owned assets, and the deregulation of financial markets, with further gains as these measures were adopted and spread by the Bretton Woods institutions.

The resulting "liberal international order," often lauded as "rules-based," now serves gargantuan and increasingly footloose firms in their endless pursuit of higher rents in heavily concentrated markets across the globe. The result is a polarized world economy in which instability and insecurity have become the norm for more and more households in rich and poor countries alike.

There are three pictures of what the neoliberal economic order now looks like that we think will

Figure 1.1 The Elephant Curve: Global Income Distribution and Real Income Growth, 1980–2016

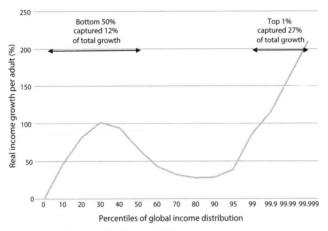

Source: World Inequality Report 2020

help illuminate the scale of the problem and the urgent action that is needed. The first is what has become known as the "Elephant Curve," designed by the former World Bank economist Branko Milanovic. Figure 1.1 reproduces that figure, showing how the top 1 percent of the global income spectrum has captured 27 percent of total growth since 1980, while the bottom 50 percent captured just 12 percent over the same period – and the fact that the latter amount was gained by developing countries is largely explained by the rise of China and India. The middle classes in the United States and Europe, and the vast majority of the world's poor, have felt their incomes squeezed.

The second picture is a figure we created for an earlier report and dubbed "The Crocodile Graph." Shaped like the jagged mouth of that rapacious reptile, this figure exhibits the top 2,000 multinational corporations' profit in terms of percentage point change of GDP, versus the global labor share of income.

The World Inequality Lab estimates that since 1980 inequality has risen or remained extremely high nearly everywhere in the global economy, with some of the sharpest rates of increase occurring in India and China and among emerging-market and developing countries, showing that even in the places where larger aggregate growth has occurred it is not shared across the population (World Inequality 2020).

The third picture is the Weather, Climate, and Catastrophe Index. The twenty-first century has been marked by climate-related natural catastrophes that have posed great economic risks to the world economy, and the risks are rising each year. There has been an increased incidence of floods, droughts, heatwaves, and fires globally that has cost hundreds of billions of dollars on an annual basis. The price tag for these events has been upwards

Figure 1.2 The Crocodile Graph: Top 2,000 Transnational Corporations' Profit and Global Labor Income Share (Percentage Point Change of GDP)

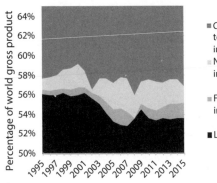

A. Global functional income distribution around the split

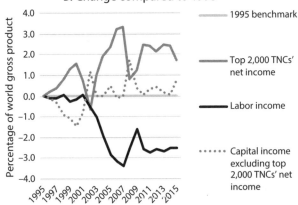

Source: UNCTAD 2017

13

Figure 1.3 Economic Losses from Extreme Weather

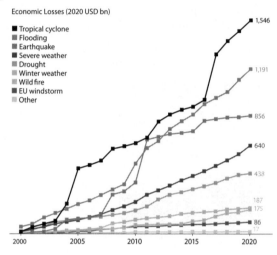

Economic Losses (2020 USD bn)

- Tropical cyclone
- Flooding
- Earthquake
- Severe weather
- Drought
- Winter weather
- Wild fire
- EU windstorm
- Other

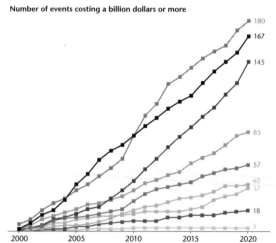

Number of events costing a billion dollars or more

Source: Climate, Weather, and Catastrophe Insight 2021

14

of $6 trillion in this century. Just one event in Dominica in 2017 caused over 200 percent of GDP in economic damage, while the cost for just the first half of 2021 was $298 billion, showing that the climate crisis is bringing major economic costs as we speak.

Rewriting the Rules of the International Economic Order

According to the IMF managing director, Kristalina Georgieva, "we face a new Bretton Woods *moment*" (Georgieva 2020). The *Financial Times* (April 3, 2020) concurs: in its call for radical reforms to reverse the policy direction of the past four decades and establish a new social contract that works for all, the international dimension is embraced and the parallel with the Bretton Woods moment of 1944 acknowledged. But unlike then, reforms have the actually existing multilateral system to contend with. The global economic order needs a reset that scales back unduly intrusive global rules in some areas and expands the system in others, in order to provide a broader set of global public goods and to align international cooperation with economic, social, and environmental goals that require a better mix of international resources and national policy autonomy.

With this backdrop in mind, we co-convened a series of roundtables in Geneva and Boston in 2018 and 2019 – including diplomats, experts and scholars, civil society organizations, union representatives, and former and current government officials – to articulate a set of design principles for a new multilateralism. We titled these principles the "Geneva Principles for a Global Green New Deal":

- Global rules should be calibrated toward the overarching goals of social and economic stability, shared prosperity, and environmental sustainability and be protected against capture by the most powerful players.
- States should share common but differentiated responsibilities in a multilateral system built to advance global public goods and protect the global commons.
- The right of states to policy space to pursue national development strategies should be enshrined in global rules.
- Global regulations should be designed both to strengthen a dynamic international division of labor and to prevent destructive unilateral eco-

nomic actions that prevent other nations from realizing common goals.
• Global public institutions must be accountable to their full membership, open to a diversity of viewpoints, cognizant of new voices, and have balanced dispute resolution systems.

With a renewed set of national goals and global public goods (outlined in Table 1.1), and guided by the Geneva Principles, this short book draws on the work of the United Nations Conference on Trade and Development (UNCTAD) and the academic literature to make the case that the international economic order needs to be fundamentally reformed to align itself with and support these new goals and ambitions. After this short introduction, Chapter 2 puts the international economic order in its proper historical context, tracing the collapse of the liberal order after World War One, the construction and rise of the embedded liberal order, and the rise and fall of neoliberalism. Chapter 3 focuses on how the neo-liberal order has made the international monetary and financial system more unstable and asymmetric. Chapter 4 traces the rise of neoliberalism in the World Trade Organization (WTO) and in the broader trade and investment treaty regime. Chapter 5 discusses the evolution of development banking.

The Case for a New Bretton Woods

Table 1.1 Policy Instruments for a New Bretton Woods

Renewed national goals and global public goods	
Bretton Woods 1.0	*Bretton Woods 2.0*
National goals	
Full employment	Full and decent employment
Structural transformation	Green structural transformation
Catch-up growth	Stable growth
Social security and welfare	Equality and justice
Policy autonomy	Decarbonization
	Resilience
	Policy autonomy
Global public goods	
Stable monetary and exchange rate system	Financial stability
	Relative global equality
Lender of last resort	Counter-cyclical and long-run finance
Counter-cyclical and long-run finance	Lender of last resort and debt authority
Open trade during recessions	Balanced trade
International cooperation	Stable global climate
	International cooperation

These chapters provide a critical analysis of the scale, governance, and performance in each of these areas of the original Bretton Woods order, and offer concrete policies for reform that are guided by the Geneva Principles. Table 1.1 provides an illustrative list of these policies to foreshadow the discussion.

The scale of the challenge of turning a global system away from fossil fuels and outsized financial interests toward mobilizing investment for a just transition to a sustainable future of clean production, economic equality, and social and environmental resilience should not be underestimated. However, on many broad macroeconomic criteria (investment shares, public spending, tax rates, wage and productivity growth, etc.), the challenge is to return to figures that were commonplace in the initial Bretton Woods era, at least in the advanced economies. A more stable international monetary and financial system with adequate liquidity provision and new mechanisms for handling sovereign debt problems would lessen the need for emerging-market and developing countries to accumulate massive foreign exchange reserves and would help lengthen investment horizons. Closing tax loopholes, shifting taxes and tariffs toward fossil fuels, and introducing regulations that steer private finance toward public goals will create plenty of resources to harness the transition through increased fiscal space, development finance institutions and multilateral development Banks (MDBs), and new commercial sector instruments. A much higher degree of coordination is required for the kind of big investment push we see as essential to moving towards real resilience. We suggest that a Global Marshall Plan can provide that push, but with room for stronger regional economic arrangements.

Finally, the trading system has to be aligned with a renewed set of national goals and global public goods. The current system accommodates market concentration, protects footloose finance, and favors rent-seeking interests in fossil fuels, banking, and pharmaceuticals, to name a few. Under its watch, corporate profits have soared as the labor share of global income has declined. Given this, the most important reform will be to introduce a competition body into the trading system to tame market concentration and ensure that the system does not favor outsized firms – while rolling back the investment and intellectual property rules that currently favor those firms. We will need to dramatically increase tariffs on fossil fuels and drop fossil fuel subsidies, while shifting to low tariffs and high subsidies for green energy and industry. There will also need to be financing for those communities, entrepreneurs, and supply chains stranded in the transition, and new governance mechanisms that include multiple stakeholders.

2

The Origins and Antinomies of the Multilateral System

The failure of the League of Nations to meet the interconnected governance challenges of sovereignty, leadership, and distribution was uppermost in the minds of the negotiators who gathered at Bretton Woods in 1944. In a profound break with their predecessors, discussions around a dedicated international financial architecture were premised on the assumption that the modern state was willing and able to undertake the challenges of attaining higher standards of living, full employment, and a fair distribution of the gains from economic progress. Moreover, politicians and policy-makers across countries (and the political spectrum) recognized that in order to achieve these goals, and to ensure that finance was the servant, rather than the master, of their economic destiny, it would be essential to extend the public realm (and policy) to the international sphere.

The partial success and subsequent unraveling of those efforts set the stage for the emergence of todays' hyperglobalized world dominated by unregulated flows of finance alongside the increasingly concentrated power of international business. In this respect at least, the current conjuncture bears some worrying parallels with the 1920s, including a multilateral system in poor shape to tackle the global challenges. This chapter offers a short detour through history in order to understand how we reached this state of affairs.

The Inter-War Years: From Reglobalization to Building Back Worse

At the end of World War One, financial interests acted quickly to restore "market confidence" to the center of economic policy-making and hasten a return to "normalcy" (James 2001: 25). This effectively meant not just a rapid dismantling of wartime controls, but an unqualified commitment to the gold standard, fealty to the professional expertise of (independent) central bankers, and the pursuit of austerity policies, all of which reduced the possibilities of moving toward a more managed economy that could deliver on the promises made by political leaders during the war and its aftermath. From the mid-1920s financial interests saw further gains from the surge of short-term capital flows, leading to an increasingly skewed pattern of income distribution in many countries (Kumhof et al. 2013).

Financial interests also defined what was the right international policy response, including in the newly established League of Nations (Mazower 2013: 150–1; Boyce 2009). Their strategy rested on an ingrained sense that pre-war stability – the Victorian "great moderation" – had derived from the infallibility of market forces and the virtues of the gold standard, not only as a self-equilibrating system for balancing international payments but as a guarantor of investor confidence, a check on government action, and a moral compass for policy-makers (Polanyi 1944: 27).[1]

In practice, the pre-war economic stability had depended on Britain's hegemonic role as champion of a stable international currency system linked to the fixed convertibility of sterling into gold and free-flowing movements of capital, along with its dogged willingness to keep its own markets open,

---

[1] On the chequered economic performance of the gold standard before 1914, see Cooper 1982.

constrain government spending (even as others did not reciprocate), and lead a coordinated response among the major central banks when the system came under serious stress (Eichengreen 2008).

At the end of the war, hampered by a weakened industrial base and the financial burden of its military efforts, Britain was not in a position to resume that role. With much of Europe absorbed by post-war reconstruction and ongoing security concerns, and the United States unwilling (and in important respects unable) to take on the hegemonic role, the dangers of an uncoordinated and unbalanced recovery in trade and capital flows loomed large (Kindleberger 1973; Tooze 2014). The League's attachment to liberalism kept it singularly focused on cutting government spending, wages and tariffs to restore these flows, which, while partially successful, left it oblivious to the consequences of the rising indebtedness and hot money that glued the system together, and ill-prepared to deal with the economic collapse that engulfed much of the globe at the end of the 1920s.[2] In the absence of

[2] Contrary to a good deal of economic history, the disruption and damage of the inter-war era was not caused by retreat and closure. Not only was economic liberalism still the dominant ideology in the 1920s, but world trade had surpassed its 1913 level by 1924 and capital flows (albeit short-term in nature) mushroomed.

clear leadership, cooperation to address chronic international imbalances was, instead, left to ad hoc arrangements between the leading economic powers (Temin and Vines 2013: chapter 2).

The lack of either a "benevolent" hegemon or robust international institutions that could foster cooperation made the international transmission of adverse shocks easier, and paved the way for a global depression (Kindleberger 1973). The economic stumblings of the League were finally ended at the 1933 World Economic Conference in London by the newly elected president of the United States (Boyce 2009).

Franklin Roosevelt was an unlikely standard bearer for radical change. He came from a patrician New York family, had a record of cautious economic management as governor of the state, and had chided Hoover for budget profligacy during the election campaign. But he understood that mass unemployment posed a threat to economic and political stability and that the appropriate response required a transformation not only at home but also internationally, through a set of economic rules and practices different from those designed to please footloose capital (Katznelson 2013: chapter 7). Progress would require abandoning the gold standard, which Roosevelt did in June 1933, and taking on Wall Street, which he did through a series of banking reforms. Along with an array of recovery, regulatory, and redistribution measures, these reforms opened the way to a broad-based experiment in managing the economy without appealing to self-correcting markets (Schlesinger 1958).

In this regard, Roosevelt's New Deal was able (and its advocates were willing) to draw on a range of unorthodox economic ideas and policies (Blyth 2002) which promoted the notion of *public service* unbeholden to private profit, in pursuit of economic security and social justice in a world of mutually dependent actors (Rauchway 2018).

Internationalizing the New Deal

The New Deal program not only abandoned the gold standard, but also broke with the wider liberal international agenda by taking on the financial elite both at home and abroad, and opened the door to an alternative narrative in support of an activist public policy agenda. While economic recovery in the United States took priority over international financial stability, the New Deal was not a simple turn to isolationism but rather a program to manage economic interdependence. A program which, its proponents understood, would have to be extended to the international sphere (Patel 2016: 4).

By the time of the Bretton Woods conference, the United States had not only consolidated its dominant position as the world's strongest economy; thanks to its recovery from the Great Depression and a booming wartime economy, it had also strengthened its institutional and political capabilities to the point that it was able to assume a hegemonic role. Its rapid buildup of military strength between 1940 and 1944 confirmed its leadership status and gave it the confidence to engage in deliberations over the design of post-war multilateral structures that, unlike after World War One, could be used to support an expanded economic and social agenda. Learning from that earlier experience, these would have to include multilateral disciplines over exchange rate policies, mechanisms for the provision of international liquidity, and restrictions on destabilizing capital flows (Helleiner 1994).

The negotiations, which kicked off as the conflict still raged, were the first in which "technicians" (rather than bankers) were in charge of shaping economic affairs (Skidelsky 2000: 182), with the institutional details fought out between John Maynard Keynes, representing the waning (colonial) power of the heavily indebted United Kingdom, and

Harry Dexter White, negotiating on behalf of the United States, the dominant industrial and creditor economy.

The IMF was created to ensure an orderly system of international payments at stable exchange rates, multilaterally negotiated and adjustable, under conditions of strictly limited international capital flows. Its most important function was to provide international liquidity, not only to avoid deflationary adjustments and trade and exchange restrictions in deficit countries, but also to help maintain stable exchange rates during temporary payments disturbances. The negotiations on institutional detail leading up to, and during, the Bretton Woods conference in 1944, which pitted Keynes's *bancor*-based international lender of last resort against White's quota-based Stabilization Fund, have been extensively documented elsewhere (Skidelsky 2000). White's scheme inevitably prevailed, in line with the greater economic and political power of the United States. This led to the establishment of a fund, with contributions from countries partly in gold and partly in their own currencies, which would be available for drawing by those in need of international reserves, but where the onus of adjustment was almost exclusively on the deficit country.

Despite the differences over institutional design, there was broad agreement that private capital on its own could not be relied upon to achieve post-war stability, and that countries would need sufficient policy space to pursue a full-employment agenda and extend social protection (Martin 2013). By implication, the newly established institutions were not to be used to impose deflationary measures on countries seeking access to their financial support. Moreover, the leading powers, in particular the United States and the United Kingdom, whose financial centers would remain dominant once the war ended, would have to be willing to forgo, or attenuate, the pursuit of their immediate economic interests in favor of a broader commitment to systemic stability. In practice these assumptions would be respected more in the breach than in the observance.

The birth of the IBRD (now the World Bank) is generally thought to have been easier than that of the IMF. But it too was contested along two important axes: whether long-term financing should be private or public, and the relative importance given to reconstruction versus development. It was broadly recognized that the terms and conditions of private financing, notably market interest rates, would not be appropriate for the conditions prevailing in the borrowing countries, and that the public investment needed to raise living standards in poorer countries would require public financing mechanisms. This feature was highly novel: no international financial institution had ever been created with the purpose of channeling resources to poorer countries. The initial drafts of the IMF Articles of Agreement prepared by White included an explicit mandate to promote "development," including through the movement of capital from "capital-rich to capital-poor countries" (Helleiner 2014: 121, 102–5). For some of the international New Dealers, the Tennessee Valley Authority, which gave financial and technical support to poor regions of the American South, provided a model (Helleiner 2014). The Europeans at Bretton Woods were, however, worried about a trade-off between financing for reconstruction and for development, and even though reconstruction was soon handed over to the Marshall Planners, White's initial impulse was compromised.

Trade issues had already provoked sharp disagreements in the run-up to the conference, particularly on the question of Britain's imperial preferences, and were dropped from negotiations. The creation of an International Trade Organization to complement the new financial institutions was instead shifted to the United Nations. Disagreements between the

United States and the United Kingdom over how quickly trade liberalization would happen persisted, with the latter making the case for more policy space in line with pressure on the UK's balance of payments, its firmer commitment to full employment, and its lingering imperial ambitions. But the active participation of developing countries on trade issues also helped to reinforce this line by bringing a development dimension into the discussions. In particular, their concerns with industrial strategy, differential treatment, and the role of multinational corporations helped keep the focus on "managed trade." In Havana in 1948 a compromise agreement was eventually reached which did incorporate some of the demands of developing countries, including infant-industry protection, commodity agreements, and the right of host countries to manage foreign direct investments, allowing for appropriation with due compensation (Graz 2014).

The Tempering of New Deal Multilateralism

By the end of World War Two the United States had built the economic, political, and military muscle to assume the role of hegemon across the world and in the Bretton Woods institutions. More importantly, through the Marshall Plan, it demonstrated a willingness to temper that dominance with wider collective responsibilities. The leadership and sovereignty challenges that had plagued the League of Nations had, it seemed, been solved (Helleiner 1994).

The ethos of New Deal internationalism was perhaps most clearly laid out by Henry Morgenthau in his pitch for the Bretton Woods agreement to the House Banking and Currency Committee in March 1945. Taking time to explain why the agreement was good for every American citizen, Morgenthau laid out three fundamental principles established at the conference for a more stable, secure, and prosperous world: avoiding imported deflation and the threat of beggar-thy-neighbor policies; supporting economic and political sovereignty through reliable access to international public finance for productive investment and liquidity provision; and disciplining economic aggression by big states and powerful private actors, particularly financial interests (Morgenthau 1945).

Between 1950 and 1973 trade and output grew at an unprecedented pace across the Western world, and the income and technological gaps that had opened up between the United States and Europe during the inter-war period began to close.

Morgenthau's principles seemed to be working well.

But while the new multilateral institutions were tasked with promoting these principles, they were not the only factors shaping the post-war multilateral order. Indeed, a gradual erosion of Morgenthau's principles began soon after his pitch to Congress, laying the basis for their abandonment in the 1970s and a new chapter of global governance from the early 1980s onwards. In this respect, the differences between Keynes and Dexter White over the internal plumbing of the IMF, while important, have tended to eclipse the differences within the US administration over the New Deal legacy for post-war international relations.

With the arrival of the more conservative Truman administration in April 1945, many of the key architects of the internationalized New Deal were marginalized, including both Morgenthau (who resigned in July) and White (who left government service in March 1947 and died shortly afterwards), while figures close to the New York financial community assumed more prominent positions in foreign and economic policy (Helleiner 2014). Since members of this community had been skeptical of the Bretton Woods plans and institutions – and of the New Deal more generally – they were soon lobbying to reduce their powers and ambition.

These officials were much more critical of state-led development policies, arguing that private investment flows and free trade should serve as the main engines of development. The leadership of the IBRD, with increasing links to Wall Street, became reluctant to extend large-scale development loans, particularly to countries that had not reached debt settlements with foreign creditors. More generally, support to developing countries shifted away from international public assistance to technical advice on domestic reforms (Helleiner 2014).

Business interests also began to push back against elements of the New Deal, including legislation on full employment and workers' rights, and to promote a more business-friendly growth strategy (Blyth 2002). With US corporations eying profitable opportunities in markets abroad, these interests mobilized against the regulatory oversight of the International Trade Organization agreed in Havana in 1947. The Truman administration did not pursue its ratification in the Senate, leaving trade negotiations in the narrower hands of the GATT (Graz 2014).

The 1950s witnessed a series of further retreats from the international New Deal, including a rehabilitation of private capital flows and a turn to greater policy conditionalities attached to lending to developing countries, prescribing tighter credit constraints, cuts in public expenditure, partial wage freezes, and repeal of subsidies as a means to combat inflation (Felix 1961). The rehabilitation of capital flows was given an even bigger boost by the creation of the Eurodollar markets which were, in effect, the result of a marriage of convenience between US-based multinationals with growing investments abroad, and a Bank of England determined to retain a stake for the City of London in international financial matters. Exploiting the constraints on US banks introduced during the 1930s at the height of the New Deal, and its own long-standing involvement with international financial transactions, the City of London became the location of choice for US corporations and banks to manage their international operations free from domestic oversight.[3] The rapid expansion of deposits in these Euromarkets in the 1960s and 1970s not only opened up a new source of private credit creation but also helped establish a fledgling network of opaque institutions that diminished national oversight of fiscal matters,

---

[3] On the history and working of these offshore markets see Norfield 2016.

corporate pricing behavior, accounting practices, etc. With much of the lending used for speculative purposes, arbitrage profits added a source of instability in the dollar-based system of fixed exchange rates (Helleiner 1994; Altamura 2017).

That system came under further pressure in the 1960s as attention shifted to the anchoring role of the dollar and the exuberant privilege it afforded the United States to run persistent current-account deficits. This left the stability of the entire exchange rate system resting on surplus countries forgoing conversion of the dollars they accumulated as reserves into gold. The threat of a dollar crisis became increasingly difficult to ignore as US spending on war and poverty alleviation mushroomed in the 1960s, blowing up its trade deficit and exposing the limits of the Fund to manage a system of pegged exchange rates – with irreversible consequences when the Nixon administration suspended the convertibility of the dollar into gold in 1971.

These mounting pressures on the international financial system coincided with weaknesses in the post-war growth model which began to emerge in the late 1960s, reflected in growing distributional struggles both within countries (between capital and labor) and across countries as commodity producers in the developing world pushed back against decades of market subordination, resulting in inflationary pressures and balance-of-payments difficulties. This heightened the ambiguities in the multilateral system and ultimately led to the collapse of the Bretton Woods system in the early 1970s. The suspension of the dollar's link to gold, followed by its abandonment in 1973, cut the IMF adrift in a world of floating exchange rates, rising capital mobility, and growing inflationary pressure. With insufficient resources to provide adequate liquidity in the system, the Fund ditched its founding principles and turned to adjustment through austerity. The commitment to full employment enshrined in Article I of its Charter was shelved, and the international role of private banks was enlarged by making them the vehicles to recycle petrodollars.

A very different approach to the management of an interdependent world economy from the one that had underpinned the post-war consensus began to take shape: flexible exchange rates, deregulated finance, and lower tariffs and taxes would become the order of the day. Making this new system work would require a very different set of principles from those promoted by the international New Dealers.

The Strange Rebirth of the Liberal International Order

The breakdown of the Bretton Woods system and the shift to floating exchange rates was expected to bring about a looser form of monetary cooperation allowing greater independence for policy-makers (at least in developed countries). Instead, as the US economy shifted away from a military-industrial complex onto a military-financial axis, the voice of organized labor was silenced as that of organized money grew louder.

Critically, the role of the dollar as the financial lodestone in a world of floating exchange rates was preserved by ensuring that Wall Street became the magnet for attracting and recycling footloose capital. Paul Volcker, Chair of the Federal Reserve between 1979 and 1987, was candid about orchestrating a "controlled disintegration in the world economy" that would preserve the exorbitant privilege of the dollar's reserve-currency status and pave the way for a much greater role for financial institutions at home and abroad, but in particular for Wall Street (Mazower 2013: 316–17). Getting there involved the Federal Reserve hiking interest rates to unprecedented levels; by the time monetary normality returned, the Bretton Woods system was well and truly buried and a liberal international economic order was in the making. Room for government action was further sacrificed for easier access to international capital markets, leaving independent central banks to coordinate on a more informal basis in response to unexpected shocks under the leadership of the Federal Reserve (Abdelal 2007). Slower growth, weak overall demand, and saturated markets led to new alliances between ever larger financial and industrial firms with unprecedented access to private credit and a growing propensity to replace long-term productive investment with rent-seeking behavior (Altamura 2017).

In the wake of this hegemonic shift, the institutional facade of the international trade and finance system established at Bretton Woods remained in place, but the interior plumbing was ripped out. In the absence of a fixed exchange rate regime, the IMF's role of advancing "monetary aid" in support of a stable international financial system geared to a "mutual rise in standards of living" (Morgenthau 1945) was transformed as it became an enabler of "an open and liberal system of capital movements" (Camdessus 1997).

By the end of the 1980s most advanced countries had opened their capital accounts, and through a combination of pressure and persuasion, emerging economies had started to open theirs to welcome foreign direct investment, which began to flow from North to South in search of higher yields. The collapse of the Soviet Union converted yet more states to the gospel of deregulation. The era of financialization was in full swing. Despite some disagreement about the pace of liberalization, the basic choice presented to all countries was unequivocal: integrate and flourish, or resist and fall further behind. At biannual gatherings of finance ministers in Washington in the 1990s, talk inevitably turned to revising the Articles of the IMF to include capital account convertibility. The endlessly repeated promise was that by unlocking private capital and unleashing the innovative impulse of financial markets, stability and prosperity would spread rapidly across the world. The Asian financial crisis that began in 1997 tempered some of these moves, but the blame was quickly shifted on to weak governance in the crisis-hit countries, allowing for further ruptures in long-standing institutional and market firewalls in the name of competition, efficiency, and innovation.

The main effect of these trends was to put credit creation ever further out of reach of regulators. Not only did banks grow massively in size and scope, but financial deregulation also created a new financial subsystem with minimal public oversight – aptly referred to as "shadow banking" – which traces its roots back to the Euromarkets and is now estimated to account for around a third of the global financial system (Shaxson 2018).

What did not happen was the emergence of a financial system geared to boosting capital formation. As financial innovation proceeded apace and state oversight and regulation were reduced, speculative financial markets flourished at the expense of credit directed to the productive sector. The result has been boom-bust cycles along with exchange rate instability and misalignments leading to sudden shifts in the pattern of international competitiveness, trade tensions, and uneven growth.

Over much the same time period, the governance of international trade has moved toward a single-tier system of rights and obligations, in which developing countries are expected, generally, to commit to a level of obligations much closer to those of developed countries, in exchange for the predictability of a "rules-based system." Boosting competitiveness through trade liberalization has been given priority over economic growth and full employment, thereby rekindling mercantilist agendas, as large international firms seek support to bend the rules in their favor.

The Case for a New Bretton Woods

A range of issues of interest to developing countries, including changes in their terms of trade, technology transfer, non-tariff barriers, and restrictive business practices, have either fallen down the negotiating agenda at the international level or disappeared altogether (UNCTAD 2011). Trade agreements, particularly at the regional and bilateral levels, have increasingly extended their reach into areas of policy previously the sole prerogative of national authorities.

Much of national and global economic policy has progressively been driven by an agenda of "deep" integration, including the elimination of non-tariff barriers to trade and capital flows and enlargement of the space in which corporations can make profits through privatization, deregulation, and flexibilization of labor markets.

In effect, the collapse of the Bretton Woods system paved the way for a new international financial and economic order built on a strong ideological faith in the inherent efficiency and stability of markets, which opened up new profit-making opportunities for an increasingly unregulated financial sector and highly concentrated forms of footloose capital. The space for countries to tailor their policies to particular histories, contexts, and institutional structures, which was at the heart of the Bretton Woods arrangements, was replaced with a one-size-fits-all agenda of so-called "sensible economic policies" which bore a close resemblance to the policy agenda of the 1920s (Temin 2010). The rapid ascent of financial interests eroded the checks and balances that had previously helped to channel market forces into the kind of productive activities needed for long-term growth. Instead, it encouraged short-term flows, and at times destructive, rent-seeking behavior by banks and businesses. These flows have produced a highly unstable environment that is subject to speculative trading, boom and bust cycles, and highly unequal patterns of income distribution. When prices inevitably fall, financial booms leave behind large debt overhangs that delay the recovery of the real economy, sometimes for decades.

In the face of these centrifugal forces, the glue holding the system together has been the explosion of private debt along with a Pandora's box of new financial instruments which Alan Greenspan promised would enhance market flexibility, ensure the smooth management of debt accumulation, and boost stability (Greenspan 2005). In reality, the emergence of this lightly regulated and privatized credit system has allowed the financial sector to transact more and more with itself, creating a complex network of closely interconnected debtor–creditor relations that harbor dangerous levels of fragility and cannot easily be re-engineered for productive investments (private or public) without a fundamental reorganization of the financial system.

The response to the global financial crisis of 2008, despite bold pronouncements at the time, failed to rein in the unchecked power of footloose capital and undertake the required reforms to the international financial architecture. A decade on, the Covid-19 pandemic has caused the largest global recession since the end of World War Two and further exposed, and intensified, the inequities and fragilities of the hyperglobalized world that emerged from the ashes of the Bretton Woods system. It has again demonstrated the incapacity of a liberalized international governance architecture to respond to a global crisis with effective, coordinated, and inclusive global policy and action. If the recovery from the pandemic is to avoid stretching the economic gaps within and across countries to political breaking point, as well as bring us back from the brink of a climate catastrophe, big changes to that architecture will be needed. The next chapters lay out what those changes should be.

3

Building Back a Better International Monetary and Financial System

In an interdependent global economy, a stable international monetary and financial system helps support growth by mitigating economic shocks, extending investment horizons, and supporting a stable trading system. By most authoritative accounts, for their first quarter-century of existence the arrangements established at Bretton Woods "functioned more or less as planned" (Eichengreen 2008: 92). Global growth hit new highs, international trade expanded, and financial stability was maintained, allowing governments in the North to focus on delivering full (or at least high) employment and extending welfare programs.

As described in the previous chapter, however, the Bretton Woods system never lived up to the aspirations of the international New Dealers, hamstrung as it was by the pushback of organized capital in the

United States and by the tensions arising from making the dollar the lodestone of the fixed exchange rate system. Development concerns, in particular, were crowded out. Efforts in the 1970s to forge a more inclusive multilateralism eventually faltered in the face of resistance from a United States determined to maintain its hegemonic status as it transitioned into a post-industrial economy. The forces of hyperglobalization this helped unleash proved strongest, and the direction of global governance has since aligned the challenges around global governance with the needs of private footloose capital. This was made possible by preserving the central role of the dollar in international economic transactions, backed by deep financial markets and the world's most powerful central bank. However, the hegemonic role of the United States has subsequently been exposed to the increasing economic turbulence and growing social and political divisions of its own highly financialized economy, and to newly emerging poles of influence abroad, including the consolidation of the European Union and the reemergence of China as a global player.

If trends continue along current lines, the global economy will not make the transformational changes needed to address the compounding economic, social, and environmental challenges that are threatening people, communities, and the planet. As in 1944, we should be under no illusion that tinkering with the existing international monetary system will be sufficient to provide the global public goods or the international coordination necessary to foster stability, equality, and sustainable prosperity in the twenty-first century.

The Breakdown of the International Monetary System

Building back better was at the heart of the New Deal's response to the Great Depression and its internationalization was at the heart of the governance challenges that framed negotiations at Bretton Woods a decade later. Monetary and financial instability had been a major trigger of the Depression and there were no illusions that going back to the earlier system would be the right course of action for a world committed to "the promotion and maintenance of high levels of employment and real income and to the development of the productive resources of all members as primary objectives of economic policy" (IMF 2020).

In the current context, any investment and growth regime must be consistent with meeting the internationally agreed Sustainable Development Goals (SDGs), including using energy more efficiently and rapidly reducing its carbon content. Doing so will require a coordinated investment push on an unprecedented scale, in the order of an additional two to three percentage points of global GDP annually for the foreseeable future (UNCTAD 2019; Bhattacharya et al. 2019; Pollin 2020). It is therefore imperative that the international system supports domestic mobilization efforts, including the requisite fiscal space in countries at all levels of development, and provides the financial stability needed to bend investment decisions to a longer time horizon.

There is a broad recognition that the turn to hyperglobalization has, with the exception of China, failed to produce a sustained rise in capital formation. The literature is clear that there is no robust relationship between capital openness and economic growth, especially in emerging-market and developing countries that have not reached a threshold of institutional strength (Jeanne et al. 2012; Furceri et al. 2019). Figure 3.1 indicates how detached global finance has become and why there is a weak link between finance and growth.

The literature is also clear that hyperglobalization is strongly associated with banking and financial

Figure 3.1 Runaway Finance vs Real Investment

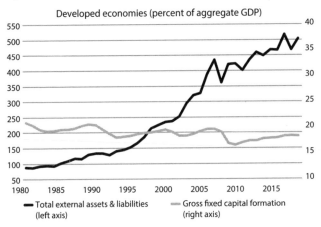

Developed economies (percent of aggregate GDP)

— Total external assets & liabilities (left axis)   — Gross fixed capital formation (right axis)

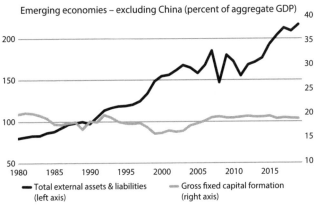

Emerging economies – excluding China (percent of aggregate GDP)

— Total external assets & liabilities (left axis)   — Gross fixed capital formation (right axis)

Source: Izurieta et al. 2018

Figure 3.2 Instability of Global Capital Flows

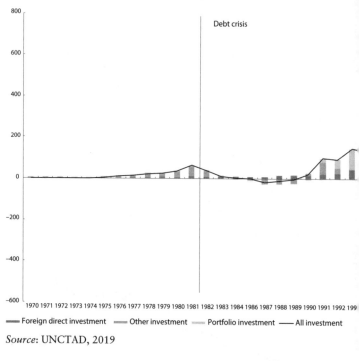

Source: UNCTAD, 2019

crises, particularly in emerging-market and developing countries, but with greater virulence and contagion when they occur in advanced economies (Jeanne et al. 2012; UNCTAD 2018). As Figure 3.2 shows, capital surges and sudden stops have been characteristic of the financial crises in Latin America in the 1980s, Mexico and East Asia in the 1990s, the dot-com and housing crises in advanced

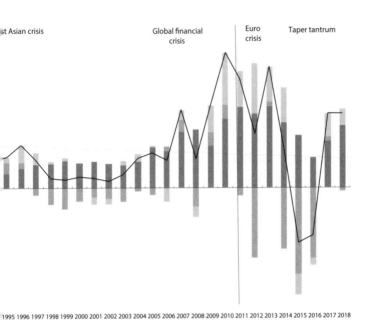

st Asian crisis

economies in the 2000s, and again in the aftermath
of the Covid-19 pandemic in 2020–1.

These crises have followed a broadly similar pattern, though the precise circumstances of the bust
vary from region to region and among individual
countries. The inherent instability in the global
dollar-based system is closely linked to periods
of expansionary and contractionary policy in the

United States. When the United States lowers interest rates there is a surge of financialized capital into world markets that fuels global debt binges, frenzied mergers and acquisitions, short-term asset booms, and appreciates exchange rates in countries across the world. When there is a tightening of policy those dollars suddenly stop flowing and reverse course back to the "safety" of the United States, depreciating currencies and triggering debt spirals, recessions, and drags on global growth (Jeanne et al. 2012; Akyuz 2017). The danger was recognized by the original framers of the IMF, who in early drafts of its articles allowed for capital flows to be regulated from both capital source and receiving countries, only to see the former eliminated under pressure from the banking sector (Gallagher 2015).

Financial globalization is also strongly associated with inequality and, as Keynes recognized from his experience in the 1930s, with rising rentier incomes. When combined with the higher propensity to save of the wealthier classes, this adds to macroeconomic imbalances through insufficient aggregate demand (underconsumption) and excessive financial gambling that favors short-term speculative activities over productive investment. The result then, as now, is an increasingly polarized and fragile global economic system, with instability feeding inequality feeding more instability, leading to vulnerability to shocks. This is especially true in countries and sectors where labor laws are loose and firms can lay off workers during times of financial instability (Furceri et al. 2019; Gallagher et al. 2019).

Having abandoned the task of controlling unruly capital flows, the response of international financial institutions to these threats has been to promote the idea of a "Global Financial Safety Net" (GFSN), consisting of currency swaps and ad hoc liquidity provisioning, regional financial arrangements, soft regulations (Basel Accords, Financial Stability Board, etc.), and national country policies such as reserve management. However, there are clear differences across countries in terms of crisis response. When crises pose threats to the advanced economies and the United States itself, the Federal Reserve Bank has adopted an aggressively expansionary monetary policy, lowered interest rates, and engaged in currency swaps with selective central banks. The rest of the world, by contrast, must either seek to roll over existing debts at higher interest rates, draw on their own reserves, or turn to the IMF, which has tended to condition such support on contractionary policies. The overwhelming evidence suggests that these policies do not trigger growth but stifle investment, accentuate inequality, and increase poverty, putting a general drag on the world economy and diverting global efforts to mobilize finance for climate and development goals (see Kentikelenis et al. 2016).

In order to buffer themselves from financial volatility, emerging-market and developing countries do all they can to accumulate dollar reserves so they can intervene in foreign exchange markets rather than go to the IMF. This "self-insurance" entails a massive transfer of wealth from developing to developed countries through the purchasing of dollar reserves, and accentuates global imbalances whereby some countries have oversized current-account balances, causing others to have ever larger deficits. At upwards of $6 trillion, these reserves carry significant social costs on the domestic front as well, diverting finance from more productive investment (Akyuz 2017). Despite using some or all of these measures, many countries have still fallen into crisis and been forced to restructure their debts through existing arrangements which favor private creditors, thereby prolonging the downturn. Collectively this leads to a "contractionary bias" in the international monetary system (Ocampo 2018) which is antithetical to delivering the SDGs.

Holes in the Safety Net

The international monetary and financial system is failing to steer finance toward productive investment that enhances our climate and development goals. Worse, it is inherently unstable, accentuates inequalities, and puts a drag on global economic growth. The reasons for this fall into three categories. First is the continuing undue reliance on the dollar and the inadequate liquidity support from international financial institutions. Second is the asymmetric governance and coordination across the system. These factors compound a third factor, which is the lack of effective policy-making, and blind spots or gaps that are not being addressed at all. Each of these will be addressed in turn in this section.

One of the core sources of global financial instability is an over-reliance on the US dollar as a global means of exchange and store of value. As noted earlier, dollar hegemony is a key cause of financial volatility by triggering massive "waves" of debt that surge during periods of expansionary monetary policy and stop during contractions and other shocks. The danger of dollar hegemony is exacerbated by the weakness of financial regulation in the United States and on a global level. Contrary to its original articles, capital controls have been delegitimized by the IMF, if not completely banned, despite their proven value (Abdelal 2007; Gallagher 2015).

Expert opinion is divided about the sustainability of dollar hegemony. Empirical views on this matter emphasize the continued large share of dollars in global foreign reserves, in banks' foreign currency assets and liabilities, and in world trade invoiced in dollars. Others consider that multipolar systems of international monetary governance, rather than their dominance by a single leading currency, have been the longer historical rule and will reemerge. An additional and rather different challenge arises from the creation and expansion of private money – or cryptocurrencies – in the international arena, using new technologies. The available evidence for developing countries would suggest that dollar hegemony remains well entrenched.

There is still an argument to be made for supplanting the dollar with a new global reserve currency (Stiglitz et al. 2010; Ocampo 2018). We are sympathetic to this view but do not see it as practical or possible in the crucial decades ahead. Part of the reason why the dollar remains the world's currency is the lack of viable alternatives. Whereas the euro, the yen, the British pound, and the renminbi are global currencies, each is dogged by weaknesses that will take decades to resolve if they are to match the dollar's status (Eichengreen 2012; Prasad 2015, 2016). Nor is a regime of multiple (including digital) currencies optimal either. Multiple currencies bring diversification to the system, but they also add a new source of instability given the exchange rate volatility across currencies held as reserve assets (Stiglitz et al. 2010).

Instead, and as discussed below, an increased use of the IMF's "Special Drawing Rights" (SDRs) provides a more immediate option for piercing dollar hegemony. While the deregulation of financial markets was expected to increase economic efficiency, that has not really happened. Rather, as Korinek and Kreamer (2014) have illustrated, the so-called "efficiency" of the deregulated financial sector has come at the cost of efficiency in the real productive economy. While larger financial and corporate players can make significant gains from excessive risk-taking in a deregulated financial environment, the real economy is impacted by a higher incidence of credit crunches and the lack of a stable supply of credit. As discussed in the previous section, the lack of financing has held back a green transition and is accentuating inequalities within nations.

As it has evolved, the GFSN has failed to reach not only the requisite scale but also policy effectiveness.

What is more, there are glaring gaps in the coverage of the system, and its governance has remained unduly asymmetric.

Given that most countries are shut out from bilateral currency swaps and must resort to the IMF or regional financial arrangements, there is just $2 trillion available in emergency liquidity finance in the world economy, with just $696 billion available for emerging-market and developing countries (see Table 3.1; Gallagher et al. 2020). Very few countries have access to bilateral currency swap lines (Mehrling 2015). Many countries are concerned that they did not have access to this type of support – either because they did not qualify given *ex ante* conditionality criteria, or because of more arbitrary geopolitical criteria (Aizenman and Pasricha 2010; Mehrling 2015).

Collectively, regional financial arrangements (RFAs) have approximately $1 trillion in liquidity with just $329 billion available for emerging-market and developing countries. Some RFAs are in the form of swap arrangements (such as the Chiang Mai Initiative and the BRICS Contingent Reserve Arrangement) or credit facilities (the Latin American Reserve Fund, the European Stability Mechanism, and the Arab Monetary Fund). While RFAs are more flexible and have more "ownership" over

Table 3.1 Multilateral and Regional Liquidity Facilities in the World Economy

	Lending/swap capacity (billion USD)	Non-OECD share of lending capacity
International Monetary Fund	971.1	388.5
European Stability Mechanism	547.7	0.0
Chiang Mai Initiative Multilateralization	240.0	201.6
Contingent Reserve Arrangement	100.0	85.0
European Financial Stabilisation Mechanism	67.7	0.0
EU Balance of Payments Facility	54.1	0.0
North American Framework Agreement	14.0	0.0
Eurasian Fund for Stabilization and Development	8.5	8.5
Arab Monetary Fund	3.6	3.6
Latin American Reserve Fund	6.8	6.8
European Macro-Financial Assistance Facility	2.0	0.0
South Asian Association for Regional Cooperation	2.0	2.0
Total	2,017.5	696.0

their policies, they lack adequate levels of capital, and those that require a parallel IMF program are not sufficiently used because of the general stigma associated with IMF conditionality. Thus many of them lay dormant during the crises of the 2000s (Kentikelenis et al. 2016).

The IMF is the only multilateral source of emergency liquidity in the world economy. However, its balance sheet has not kept pace with the growing size of the global economy and financial system. The IMF's $1 trillion (of which only $388 billion is available to the emerging-market and developing countries who need the Fund most) is just over 1 percent of the world economy and a miniscule percentage of the entire financial system (Kentikelenis et al. 2016).

The IMF has been hard-pressed to increase its resources, in part because its governance is biased toward the advanced economies – especially the United States and the European Union. Moreover, major IMF decisions require a supermajority of 70 or 85 percent of the vote, with voting shares calculated by a formula based largely on the size of a country's economy, its level of integration with the world economy, and the amount of foreign exchange reserves it holds. This has allowed the United States, with over 16 percent of the voting share, to maintain its veto over major policy changes. EU members collectively hold 30 percent of voting share and thus have major sway at the Fund as well. Given that future quota reform may jeopardize the veto power of the United States, increases in IMF resources through quotas have been minimal. Since the days of Bretton Woods, rather than a merit-based selection process, there has always been a "gentleman's agreement" that the managing director of the IMF would always be a European (and the World Bank president a citizen of the United States).

The quota system in general has long been a major concern for emerging-market and developing countries, who argue that they have little say over operations and program design even though they are the countries that use the IMF the most (Mohan and Kapur 2015). Although the IMF is tasked to follow a "doctrine of economic neutrality" (Swedberg 1986), case studies and statistical analysis have found that lending (and design) decisions often reflect the geopolitical and economic interests of its main shareholders, and of the United States in particular (Copelovitch 2010; Dreher et al. 2015). The result has been that the programmatic positions taken by the IMF favor large creditor countries and the financial interest groups within them. The resulting policies ensure that international creditors are safely paid in the midst of a crunch, but as noted earlier this comes at the expense of future stability, growth prospects, and rising inequality and poverty (Kentikelenis et al. 2016).

The IMF's other chief function takes the form of "surveillance" and advice where the fund monitors countries to prevent and mitigate instability. Traditionally, IMF surveillance activities have been focused almost exclusively on domestic "fundamentals" while ignoring or downplaying external shocks such as capital flow volatility, the rise of shadow banking and, until recently, climate change (Moschella 2012; Ghosh et al. 2018; Volz and Ahmed 2020). Moreover, the Fund's modeling approaches to estimating debt sustainability have a long history of producing erroneous projections (on the optimistic side) that lead to extended use of IMF facilities and decreases in host country welfare (Guzman and Heymann 2015; EPG 2018).

As Anne Krueger, the IMF's first deputy managing director, lamented in 2001, "we lack incentives to help countries with unsustainable debts resolve them promptly and in an orderly way" (Krueger 2001). She called this one of the most "glaring gaps" in the international financial system. Since that time there have been calls for sovereign debt restructuring instruments from other international bodies, such as UNCTAD, who made the original proposal in the aftermath of the Latin American debt crisis of the 1980s (UNCTAD 1986, 2015). To date, more modest, market-based reforms, such as Collective Action Clauses (CACs) in bond contracts, have prevailed. Despite these clauses favoring a supermajority of bondholders to undertake a debt restructuring, restructuring has continued to be difficult because of the great dispersion of bondholders and what is referred to as the "aggregation problem." Restructurings increasingly involve multiple bond issuances, and CAC provisions do not hold for collective action across multiple issuances as they only cover individual bonds. More recent "single-limb" CACs (which allow bonds to be restructured with just a single vote across a series of bonds) were meant to have alleviated this aggregation problem, but their use is still not widespread or well tested.

Debt restructuring continues to be a long and arduous case-by-case process that favors creditors over debtors (UNCTAD 2015). As shown in Figure 3.3, debt levels in developing countries have been rising at an alarming rate since the 2000s, with an increasing exposure to short-term and private debt (UNCTAD 2020). What is more, as the Covid-19 debt profiles have revealed, the composition of debt is very dispersed, making renegotiation politically

Figure 3.3 The Buildup of Global External Debt

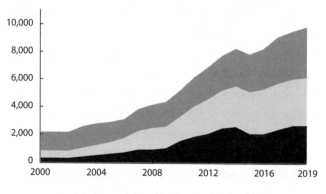

- Long-term public and publicly guaranteed debt
- Long-term private non-guaranteed debt
- Short-term debt

Source: UNCTAD 2020

cumbersome. Whereas earlier debt crises entailed bringing together the Paris Club and a small number of commercial banks, those actors now need to align not only with ever more numerous bondholders across the world, but also with large bilateral donors, such as China, that are not part of the Paris Club.

Building Back a Better System

Reforming the International Monetary System

Over the next decade a great structural transformation in the world economy will be necessary, in order to tackle the massive inequalities that have accompanied the rise of hyperglobalization, as well as steer the economy away from fossil fuels and ensure sustainable patterns of production and consumption. Nothing short of a globally coordinated investment push is required to effect this transformation, and the international monetary and financial system has to be geared to that purpose. To this end, four key reforms will be necessary: strengthening regulation of domestic and international capital flows; expanding the scale and scope of the GFSN; reforming and expanding its toolkit (especially the IMF); and reforming the governance of, and cooperation across, the system.

Regulating capital for development and climate goals

The most important component of a new Bretton Woods is the re-regulation of domestic capital markets and global capital flows so that they are aligned with our climate and development goals. As a minimum, the financial system needs to develop and deploy price- and quantity-based measures that ensure that finance flows toward productive transformation.

When designed properly, price-based incentives can not only steer finance away from socially harmful activity and toward social goals, they can also raise significant revenues during the transition. While such revenues are currently far from being widespread, over $28 billion per year is raised by fossil fuel taxes that are either re-invested in green transformations and adjustment or used to alleviate other taxes. Closing tax loopholes and introducing financial transaction taxes on short-term capital flows will help throw sand in the wheels of footloose capital (Carl and Fedor 2016; UNCTAD 2019).

Following a contentious set of deliberations after the 2008–9 crisis, the IMF officially changed its view on capital controls, going so far as to rename them "capital flow management measures" (CFMMs) in order to dampen the stigma that had become attached to "controls." Since that time, however, the IMF has been reluctant to operationalize this view, and (as will be discussed in the next chapter) numerous trade and investment treaties, as well as the OECD codes, have deemed CFMMs illegal (Gallagher 2015). The ambivalence in the use of these measures needs to end, and they need to be applied at "both ends" of the flow, as the original architects of the system recognized (Ostry et al. 2012).

The effective functioning and stability of the financial system at the international level also require better coordination among central banks. Climate-induced financial risks "could ultimately justify the implementation of measures aimed at mitigating them across all central banking operations" (Campiglio et al. 2018: 466). Moreover, in many cases, policy stances can be taken under this rationale without affecting central bank mandates, although this would involve quite fundamental changes to the technical models and assumptions used to guide bank analysis and forecasting (Bradlow and Park 2020).

Some central bankers have already started viewing this problem more technically as a "tragedy of the horizon." The time frame of most monetary stability policies is two to three years, while financial stability policies have a ten-year time frame, but climate change adaptation and transformation will require many more years. The recent establishment of a central bankers' Network for Greening the Financial System reflects these concerns, with some members already offering loans to financial institutions at below market rates in support of green lending. While this is an encouraging start, central banks could have a much bigger and bolder role in supporting green bond issuing and green finance by public banks and governments (UNCTAD 2019; Tooze 2019).

Expanding the scale and coverage of the GFSN
The GFSN is too narrow in its scope and ambition to meet the financial strains and stresses of our hyperglobalized world. This became very evident in 2020 when emerging-market and developing countries faced a $2.5 trillion shortfall, which pales in comparison to the $380 trillion in global financial markets. Four key multilateral reforms are needed at the IMF and beyond:

- Increase IMF quotas in a stepwise fashion. As a quota-based institution this is the most legitimate way to increase its resources.
- Introduce major new allocations of IMF special drawing rights (SDRs), amounting to trillions of dollars over the next decade (Ocampo 2018).
- Establish a multilateral swap facility at the IMF, unconditional and open to all member states in certain circumstances (EPG 2018; De Gregorio et al. 2018; IMF 2017).
- Establish a global debt authority with a clear set of rules for restructuring debts, including pri-

vate lending that would be independent of either creditor or debtor interests (UNCTAD 2020).

While there has been much productive innovation within regional financial arrangements, fledgling and dormant RFAs should also be scaled up (Grabel 2018). With the exception of the European Stability Mechanism, most RFAs are under-resourced (see Table 2.1). As some of the newer RFAs – such as the Chiang Mai Initiative Multilateralization (CMIM) and the 'contingent reserve arrangement' (CRA) – become more established they should de-link from the need to have an associated IMF program so that they will be more attractive to members. There are many countries that lack access to an RFA altogether. The area of most concern here is Africa. The continent negotiated an "African Monetary Fund" over a decade ago, in some ways making it "shovel-ready"; yet it has only been signed by a handful of members and remains dormant (Dagah et al. 2019). Other gaps need to be filled in Central and South America, South Asia, and beyond (Gallagher et al. 2020).

Expand and reform the crisis-fighting toolkit
The uneven use, poor performance, and perceived stigma of the IMF's toolkit underscore the need to

revisit the design of its existing instruments and to expand the toolkit itself. As noted earlier, the lack of legitimacy of the IMF has triggered self-insurance-driven reserve accumulation that is costly, perpetuates global imbalances, and absorbs resources that could be much better deployed for more productive investment.

First and foremost, IMF country programs should abandon their contractionary bias and instead be designed to be counter-cyclical and fully aligned with development and climate goals. Better coordination of its programs with other development finance institutions could strengthen this counter-cyclical orientation. Where necessary, the IMF should devise "social protection tools" and introduce climate change metrics to mitigate any potential unintended consequences of its programs (Ortiz 2018; Volz and Ahmed 2020).

Second, the IMF will need to revamp its surveillance and advice functions not only to better help members identify and prepare for external shocks, but also to better coordinate macroeconomic policies and continue to mobilize financial resources and expand fiscal space in normal times to meet climate and development goals.

Given the degree of global interdependence, the stability of exchange rates and payment positions calls for a minimum degree of coherence among the macroeconomic policies of the systemically important countries. But the existing modalities of IMF surveillance and disciplines – unlike in the WTO – do not include ways of attaining such coherence or dealing with unilateral impulses resulting from changes in the monetary and exchange rate policies of these countries. Given the pivotal role of the dollar, global arrangements for a stable exchange rate system are not on the immediate agenda. However, regional mechanisms might warrant closer attention as a means of providing a degree of collective defense against systemic failures and instability.

The IMF will certainly need to improve its surveillance and advice on capital flow volatility. It has taken steps in the right direction but needs to acknowledge that capital flow management measures should be standard parts of the toolkit rather than a last resort in times of major instability. The Fund should also broaden its focus on the potential sources of financial stress and fragility to include the "shadow banking system," and should increase its surveillance of the potential spillover impacts of advanced-economy policies – especially US Federal Reserve policy – on capital flow volatility. Finally, it should create mechanisms to facilitate international policy coordination on managing capital flows at "both ends" across regions and between emerging-market and developing countries and advanced economies (Gao and Gallagher 2019).

In relation to these challenges, the IMF needs to radically improve its data transparency and debt sustainability analysis to account for capital flow volatility and climate change risks. Fund members should share their data on external debts in an open and transparent manner as specified under the IMF-World Bank Debt Sustainability Framework and Debtor Reporting System. IMF staff will also need to rework their modeling approaches to debt sustainability to better reflect demand-side and climate risks (Guzman and Heymann 2015; Volz and Ahmed 2020).

Reform governance and global cooperation
Alongside significant quota increases at the IMF, there must be a corresponding adjustment in the quota shares that better balances representation in decision-making so as not to drown out the voices of small developing states (Mohan and Kapur 2015; De Gregorio et al. 2018). Furthermore, the IMF should introduce an open merit-based selection process for appointing its managing director. The long-standing tradition of the IMF being directed

by a European and the World Bank by a citizen of the United States is outdated and contributes to the lack of legitimacy associated with these essential multilateral institutions (Gao and Gallagher 2019).

Whereas developed countries account for only 17 percent of voting strength in the United Nations, 24 percent in the WTO, and 34 percent in the International Fund for Agricultural Development (IFAD), they account for over 61 percent in the Bretton Woods institutions. And a single country holds virtual veto power over important decisions such as capital increases or SDR allocations.

The inclusion of developing countries in discussions of financial reform that take place outside the Bretton Woods institutions, such as at G20 summits, is a welcome step but is severely flawed in that it still excludes the vast majority of countries. Nor does the G20 possess any mechanisms for reporting or accountability to the broader international community. The simplest way to make progress on this front would be to have the G20 report to the Economic and Social Council of the United Nations.

Building back a better international monetary and financial system does not mean abandoning the institutions that were put in place over seventy-five years ago. Reform is possible, through stronger regulation of financial flows, a stepwise increase in the scale of balance-of-payment and liquidity support, and changes to governance and policies that move the system from ensuring safety in the wake of shocks to systemic financial support and stability. The changes will not, however, come from enlightened technocrats or the community of nations in the spirit of collective action. As in 1944, building back a better international monetary and financial system will require new alliances, domestically and across nations, to align the system with our climate and development goals.

4

Re-aligning the Trade and Investment Regime

While much of the rise in inequality and economic insecurity scarring the lives of people and communities across the world can be traced to the augmented position of footloose capital, much of the popular backlash against hyperglobalization – from the Battle in Seattle to the fight against vaccine apartheid – has been aimed at the international trade regime in general and the WTO in particular.

This is, in part, a result of the undue influence of economists who are pre-programmed to see trade as the anima of the contemporary global economy, and of the cavalier use of "free trade" by politicians and pundits to describe, and celebrate, the contemporary global landscape. It also has much to do with shifting geopolitical currents and particularly the rise of China on the back of its successful export-oriented development model – also invariably, but wrongly, attributed to the virtues of free trade.

In reality, the contemporary trading system has become a shock absorber of the economic and political tensions originating from the unregulated flows of footloose capital, but it has also added to those tensions thanks to its own distinct legal framework and disciplines that restrict the room for elected governments to manage those flows. As discussed in Chapter 2, the architects of Bretton Woods were in no doubt that managing the movement of money and capital would be good for international trade. Even after the United States had quietly buried the International Trade Organization, efforts to boost trade through negotiated tariff reductions in the GATT were largely a matter for advanced countries who were themselves wary of giving away too much of their policy space and remained highly protective of key parts of their economies (Rodrik 2011). These same countries were, however, reluctant to give developing countries any special support to help them benefit from participation in the international trading system.

Efforts by developing countries to reform the rules and principles of international trade to better meet their specific needs began with the creation of UNCTAD in 1964 and continued with negotiations, launched at the United Nations General Assembly in 1974, for a new international economic order. These efforts were halted in the early 1980s and then abandoned due to a combination of debt crises in the South, the growing influence of neoliberal policy advice, and Volcker's "controlled disintegration of the world economy."

The coalition of large banks and corporations behind Volker's efforts to deregulate markets and repurpose economic policy in support of finance capital was soon busy convincing governments in the United States and Europe to rewire the trading system in line with their growing presence in global markets. Those efforts culminated in the creation of the World Trade Organization in 1995, not just to implement and enforce the Uruguay Round Agreement, but to drive the liberalization agenda even deeper through recurrent ministerial gatherings and an active secretariat (Davies 2019).

The logic behind the pressure for trade liberalization mirrored that of financial liberalization, with the added advantage that trade bureaucrats and diplomats could call on heavy economic artillery to provide intellectual backup, and had, moreover, mastered the art of translating high theory into more popular jargon of "humanizing globalization" (Lamy 2006). The theory has, however, long suffered from the Ricardian vice of relying on radically simplified assumptions that distort our understanding of economic reality (Keen 2017), all the more so where large corporations with control over strategic (often intangible) assets shape the working of markets, thereby obscuring the huge asymmetries that characterize the way the contemporary trading system operates and the biased outcomes it delivers.

From Global Prosperity to Global Deregulation

In part because it left plenty of room to tailor economic policies to local circumstances, the GATT system was good for advanced economies, whose increasing trade with each other complemented a strong domestic growth regime. By contrast, increased trade under the WTO has yielded diminishing returns. Bradford et al. (2005) estimate that economic gains of trade liberalization to the US economy between 1947 and 2002 were upwards of $1 trillion, yet more than 90 percent of those gains occurred between 1947 and 1982. The benefits of trade deals since that time have been shrinking in the aggregate, and have flowed to the same interests that pushed hard for financial deregulation and reform of the international monetary system discussed in Chapter 3.

That reform drive was readily extended to the rules of the trading system. By the mid-1980s – as the economic recovery was picking up pace, organized labor and government oversight were retreating, and the threat of a new international economic order had passed – big Western financial firms, along with technology, pharmaceutical, and retail companies, were turning to untapped markets to reverse the profit squeeze of the previous decade. These firms set about organizing government support for new areas of advantage while rebranding unwanted regulations as "non-tariff barriers" and persuading policy-makers to use international trading rules to dismantle them while strengthening the protections for intellectual property. In the process, successive US administrations, along with their European counterparts, transformed the GATT from a treaty-based multilateral regime aimed at balancing global commerce and national economic goals into a new type of organization in support of deeper economic integration.

Even though developing countries were jarred by these proposals, they agreed to them on the promise of stable and open access to Western markets and that their own concerns about agricultural exports would be quickly addressed. Instead, once the new agreement was in place, the rich countries proposed a further round of liberalization that matched their own corporate interests. According to estimates by the World Bank, along with others using the same modeling techniques, the benefits of the WTO proposals over the past twenty years have been very small, increasing global economic output by $96 billion or just 0.23 percent of GDP. What is more, the vast majority of those benefits ($80 billion) accrued to a handful of financial, technology, and pharmaceutical firms in the advanced economies (Gallagher 2008b).

The result has been euphemistically referred to as a "grand bargain," where emerging-market and developing countries agree to a set of regulations on services, intellectual property, subsidies, investment, and beyond in order to maintain market access to advanced economies (Narlikar 2004; Garcia 2004). What essentially happened during the Uruguay Round was that a relatively small club of advanced economies, despite their lacking the skewed voting weights found in the IMF, was able to exploit its asymmetric bargaining power and market influence to persuade a much larger bloc of developing countries – many of whom had been hit very hard by the debt crisis at the beginning of the decade and were recovering slowly, if at all – to rewrite the rules for international trade to the advantage of corporations in the advanced economies (Shadlen 2005; Gallagher 2008a).

In the late 1990s and early 2000s, those economies attempted another wave of negotiations to further push a global deregulatory agenda; they were unsuccessful this time in part because the asymmetric forces that had shaped the Uruguay Round had weakened or even reversed (Gallagher 2013). Indeed, IMF data show that from 2000 to 2010, and then 2010 to 2015, emerging-market and developing countries accounted for 55 and 70 percent of the size and growth of the world economy respectively for the two time periods. The "grand bargain" was far less appealing.

The US administration under George W. Bush became particularly frustrated with its lack of influence at the WTO and devised a new strategy of "competitive liberalization." This sought to leverage market power to promote numerous bilateral and regional deals with smaller countries (with less bargaining power) that went far beyond the WTO's terms. The European Union quickly followed suit (Evenett and Meier 2008). These positions were fortified by a trade policy-making system captured by mercantilist-minded firms with a global reach and considerable lobbying power (Ingraham and Schneider 2014). The strategy of competitive liberalization has been clear: surround countries like India, South Africa, China, Malaysia, Brazil, and others with a set of deep agreements that will eventually get multilateralized under pressure. Since the establishment of the WTO, well over 2,000 regional and bilateral trade and investment agreements have been signed, the majority after 2002 (WTO 2020).

Rather than tightly regulating the financial sector to ensure money flows into productive investment and creates good jobs, as was the case in the Bretton Woods era and was permitted under the GATT regime, this new generation of trade deals has pushed for the deregulation of finance and investment. The model here was the North American Free Trade Agreement (NAFTA) between the US, Canada, and Mexico. However, subsequent research has shown that it has delivered only marginal gains to the US economy, equal to a one-time 0.08 percent increase in GDP (Caliendo and Parro 2015).

These outcomes reflect, in part, the linking of increased trade flows to the offshoring of production, propelled by an underlying shift in corporate strategy to minimize costs and maximize the capture of rents, which has, in combination with the indiscriminate application of neoliberal policies, exacerbated the unequalizing impact of trade in both developed and developing countries. What has been good for large international firms has, it turns out, not necessarily been good for the countries that host them.

This has been particularly true in the US, where the deregulation of financial markets and the evisceration of labor, welfare, and environmental protections, along with a neglect of infrastructure investment and industrial innovation (outside of military applications), have been pronounced, and defended in the name of reducing costs to make incumbent firms more globally competitive. The result has been financial instability, de-industrialization, and wage stagnation, with little possibility of replacing the jobs lost after China's entry into the WTO with well-paying alternatives (Acemoglu et al. 2016).

The emergence of China as the world's preeminent trading nation has been among the most visible changes in the global economy since the start of the Uruguay Round. However, this is not a matter of *post hoc ergo propter hoc*. Indeed, China's success stems from its following a different strategy to the one preached by the advocates of free trade. Until the turn of the century, China refrained from joining the WTO or entering into regional and bilateral trade and investment treaties and instead, like

Japan, South Korea, and others before them, fashioned a more strategic approach to integrating into the global economy built around establishing strong links between profits, investment, and exports in both foreign and domestic firms (Amsden 2001; Kroeber 2016).

China's strategy has been to invest heavily in infrastructure, use industrial policies to support diversification, and strengthen knowledge production to upgrade and innovate. China has also kept tight reigns on its financial sector and used special banks to steer credit and investment into strategic infant industries that may someday become globally competitive, rather than investing abroad in firms that are currently more competitive (Kroeber 2016). Since joining the WTO in 2000, China has also learnt, surprisingly quickly, how to use the flexibilities in the system as well as exploit its own massive scale economies to adapt its strategy to a more open environment. In many respects, China is emulating an earlier generation of late industrializers from the East Asia region, and smaller countries, including Indonesia, Vietnam, Bangladesh, and others, are now learning from China's experience in an effort to adapt their own late late-development strategies to contemporary global realities.

Re-aligning the Trade and Investment Regime

In many other developing countries, where the Washington Consensus has continued to hold sway over policy-makers, hyperspecialization has tied growth prospects to commodity booms and expanding extractive industries. More often than not, this has proved unsustainable. In other such countries, the expected spillovers from participating in the low value-added links in global value chains for manufacturing goods have not materialized, while inequality has been amplified by the proliferation of special processing zones, tighter intellectual property laws, tax breaks, and weaker regulations put in place to attract foreign direct investment. Again, economies have been stuck with a narrow economic base and in some cases have experienced "premature deindustrialization" (UNCTAD 2003; Rodrik 2015).

From Small Gains to Big Risks

If "free trade" agreements were delivering on their promise, the world economy would be more competitive, the gains from trade more widely shared, and the economic gaps within and across countries rapidly closing. This is not the case. Indeed, as the gains from trade have shrunk and been captured by a diminishing number of large firms, high economic costs and regulatory risks have been growing for governments, workers, citizens, and the environment. Nations are quickly learning that the rules they have signed up to don't allow them the policy space to put their economies on the right track, while the governance of the system, whether through the private handling of disputes or with a nod to corporate social responsibility, has been ceded to the very same footloose firms that needed to be regulated in the first place. This is particularly true of regional and bilateral trade and investment agreements that lack even the flexibilities remaining in the global trade body (UNCTAD 2014).

An aspect of the new generation of "free trade" deals that is lost to many analysts is that they are seldom any longer about trade, given that tariffs on goods trade have been close to zero for decades in all but a handful of sectors and countries. The focus instead is on rules with respect to government regulations on financial services, allowing foreign banks unlimited market share and all forms of capital to move in and out of countries "freely and without delay"; on intellectual property, including what research and development activities can be funded, the duration of patents, the widening of protection to trade secrets and what improvements to existing products merit protection; on the rights of foreign investors; and on government financial support to specific industries.

A summary of six of the most alarming impacts of this type of regulatory regime indicates just how far the governance of international trade has moved since the creation of the WTO:

- *Increasing financial instability.* As regulations on global capital flows weaken, surges and sudden stops, discussed in the last chapter, increase, banking crises become more frequent, and growth slows (Ostry et al. 2010; Jeanne et al. 2012). Moreover, global corporations have themselves become increasingly financialized, with highly leveraged balance sheets and heightened financial risks.
- *Boosting monopoly profits.* As markets have become more open, production and profits have been reallocated toward large firms with market power (UNCTAD 2018). A major driver of market concentration and rising corporate incomes is the greater protection for large innovating firms through intellectual property rules in trade and investment treaties (see Figure 4.1).
- *Lowering wages.* As large corporations have come to dominate global markets they have become

more and more inclined to use their profits to increase dividend payments and engage in buying back their own stock (Lazonick et al. 2020), at the expense of industrial jobs in advanced economies and the incomes of small entrepreneurs and farmers in developing countries (Acemoglu et al. 2016; Autor et al. 2020). While some governments, especially in advanced economies, have schemes to help the displaced retool, these are never sufficient in the face of large-scale adjustments (Hanson 2021).

- *Emptying government coffers.* By definition, trade and investment liberalization reduces the amount of tariff revenue – still a significant source of government income in many developing countries. But the hope is that taxes will be boosted by a more efficient use of resources. There is little evidence to support this hope. Instead, there is an associated increase in external government debt, which can accentuate all the instabilities discussed in the previous chapter. Revenue losses from membership of the WTO are estimated at over $60 billion annually for emerging-market and developing countries, with an additional $10 billion in annual losses due to the temporary exemption of e-commerce from tariffs and international taxation; potential loss in tax revenues due to trade misinvoicing and other illicit flows puts these numbers even higher (see Thrasher and Gallagher 2020).

- *Insufficient global demand.* Growing inequality, restricted fiscal space, and greater market concentration in both the digital and analogue worlds of business have squeezed government and household spending without boosting private investment, generating a bias toward underconsumption and fueling indebtedness. Both of these trends tend to end badly, including through heightened tensions in the international trading system (Klein and Pettis 2020).

- *Fueling global climate change.* In addition to protecting large financial, technology, and pharmaceutical companies, trade and investment treaties explicitly and implicitly protect the global fossil fuel industry. According to the IMF, direct subsidies to fossil fuels are estimated to be roughly $500 billion per year (IMF 2013). Carbon protectionism is even larger with respect to tariffs, with an implicit subsidy of $550 to $800 billion each year biased toward fossil fuels and away from clean production (Shapiro 2021). It is thus no surprise that the WTO has found that trade and investment treaties have been strongly associated with increased carbon

Figure 4.1 Payments and Receipts Related to the Use of Foreign Intellectual Property Rights (1995–2015)

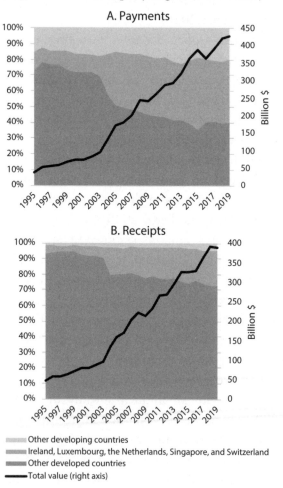

A. Payments

B. Receipts

Other developing countries
Ireland, Luxembourg, the Netherlands, Singapore, and Switzerland
Other developed countries
Total value (right axis)

Source: UNCTAD 2018

dioxide emissions, and that trade-related emissions represent about 26 percent of all global emissions (WTO-UNEP 2009).

A major problem with sub-multilateral trade and investment treaties is not just that they go beyond the WTO in constraining the policy space of advanced and developing countries alike, but that many of these treaties allow foreign firms to circumvent domestic courts and their own governments through private tribunals that have a record of siding with foreign firms over host country regulations on finance, public welfare, and the environment (Johnson et al. 2017). There have been multiple cases brought against government attempts to maintain financial stability, health-care, and pharmaceutical monopolies, and against policies to boost wages and for racial equality. Table 4.1 offers an illustrative list of cases in each of these issue areas.

A major concern moving forward is that the Investor–State Dispute Settlement (ISDS) system now in place will be a significant barrier over the coming decades to the decarbonization drive that is imperative if the world economy is to be made compatible with a livable planet. There are twenty companies in the world economy that are

Table 4.1 ISDS v Public Welfare in the World Economy, Illustrative List

Financial stability	Sovereign debt restructuring in Greece and Argentina
	Too-big-to-fail regulations in Czech Republic
Health care	Drug prices, patents, and pharma monopolies in Canada
Climate and environment	Mining and toxics in Peru
	Climate policy in Germany
Wages and equality	Minimum wages in Egypt
	Racial empowerment in South Africa

responsible for roughly one-third of carbon emissions, referred to as the "carbon majors." These companies are very active in ISDS arbitration. Seven of the ten largest ISDS awards to date have gone to these fossil fuel companies, such as ConocoPhilips, Occidental, ExxonMobil, and others. Table 4.2 shows the "success" of key carbon majors in the ISDS process, with them having been awarded $414 billion since 2013 for just fifteen cases (Tienhaara and Cotula 2020).

Even as Europe has taken the lead in decarbonization there are already pending cases on bans on fossil fuel extraction, coal plant restrictions, and coal phase-outs. Recent estimates indicate that 75

Table 4.2 ISDS Awards to "Carbon Majors"

Company	Carbon major rank	ISDS wins	Total award ($USB)
Chevron	2	2	77.7
ConocoPhillips	13	1	8.4
ExxonMobil	4	3	1.8
Occidental	55	2	1.8
Repsol	45	1	5
Yukos	48	5	50.1
Total	17	1	269.9

Source: Author's adaptation from Tienhaara and Cotula 2020

percent of the existing coal plants in the world economy are currently covered by at least one treaty with an ISDS case (Tienhaara and Cotula 2020).

Aligning the Trade and Investment Regime

The long-standing belief that international trade and direct investment can help establish a robust and inclusive growth path is firmly grounded in economic scholarship, and there are success stories where this has been the case. Yet, acknowledging this should not be taken as an endorsement of "free trade" or of development policy packages centered on rapid liberalization. The historical record of trade and development is an uneven one at best, and while it is evident that increased trade and direct investment flows under hyperglobalization have created opportunities for structural change and rising incomes, their realization has been confined to limited parts of the global economy and there are well-documented downside risks. Moreover, as global trade has decelerated since the global financial crisis, underlying structural weaknesses and vulnerabilities have been revealed in many countries that have adopted neoliberal policies.

Indeed, in our highly interdependent world, if aggregate demand is weak, financial instability endemic, and growth low, then trade runs the risk of creating more losers than winners. In such an environment, incentives are skewed less to boosting profitability through investment and increased productivity, and instead to boosting cost competitiveness through wage repression, crushing or buying up competitors, increasing markups, and seeking unilateral support from governments through trade protection or tax cuts. This can boost growth in the short run but will also increase tensions between countries and can end in a self-defeating spiral. The unfortunate truth is that the attempts of international corporations to enhance their market position through such strategies only make the broader economic system more fragile, since they lead to greater inequality, rising indebtedness, and, consequently, macroeconomic vulnerability.

A rebalancing of trade and direct investment flows will be needed to tackle the deep inequalities characteristic of today's hyperglobalized world and to transition toward a zero-carbon future in a just and inclusive manner. The key to successful reform lies in recognizing that the biggest sources of distortions in the trading system are increased market concentration, proliferation of anticompetitive practices, abuse of dominant market position, and corporate tax avoidance and evasion (and the power this has given to large corporations to influence and rig the rules of the game, at not only the national but also the international level).

Democratize the trading system

The multilateral trading regime needs new principles and dedicated rules that are geared toward human prosperity and a healthy planet. Such a regime must be more democratic. Regional, bilateral, and plurilateral deals have accentuated power inequities and distorted global trade. A resilient multilateral system must uphold the principle of one country, one vote. However, to be truly inclusive, support mechanisms need to be built into its operations that are not subject to the kind of arm-twisting and double standards that characterizes the current system. A new framework, perhaps in the context of WTO reform, will need to accommodate the two largest trading nations but must also broaden the space for development policy. It will need to advance proposals that progressively widen spaces for development by harnessing a virtuous cycle of increased productive investment, fair and balanced trade, and innovation-sharing for global economic growth from which all can derive benefit. In more general terms, this would imply seeing the multilateral trading regime as a mechanism by which trade globalization and the nation state are not competitors but are mutually reinforcing. This will require both rolling back elements of the multilateral trade agenda that have encroached too far into the responsibilities of the state, and adopting a more integrated approach to the different components of the multilateral architecture (UNCTAD 2014).

Delivering on the core issues of the developmental mandate of the Doha negotiations would be an easy first step toward restoring some level of trust in the trading system, with a commitment to special and differential treatment as a prerequisite for ensuring a fair outcome. As part of restoring trust, new issues, such as digital rules, should not be multilateralized until developing countries understand their development dimensions and accordingly can build up their competitiveness (Davies et al. 2021).

Make trade agreements about trade again
The case for liberalizing trade in goods like shoes and cars is reasonably straightforward. Countries that already enjoy cost advantages in such goods should have low tariffs, and countries still trying to become competitive should have the flexibility to extend protection for a certain amount of time. The end result is more competition and increased economic wellbeing. But the case for using trade deals and disciplines to force through regulatory changes on foreign investment (especially, but not only, short-term financial flows), as well as on health, the environment, and worker protections, has very little, if any, justification. The economic costs of financial crises, climate change, and unhealthy societies far outweigh the "benefits" that otherwise flow to unregulated firms.

To curtail market monopolization and corporate rent-seeking, much of the domestic regulatory structure dismantled over the past four decades needs to be restored. In addition, antitrust and antimonopoly laws will have to be updated to account for newer developments and the specific challenges of our time such as network effects in the digital economy. Doing so will require international support. Such restoration could start with the "Set of Multilaterally Agreed Equitable Principles and Rules for the Control of Restrictive Business Practices" adopted by the United Nations General Assembly in 1980. It could also take into account the more recent efforts of European Union regulators to curb the dominant positions of certain digital platforms.

Additional action regarding patents and the protection of intellectual property rights would be necessary to prevent their abuse for anticompetitive practices and to encourage and widen access to technological progress. This will require a review of the balance between rules on IPR protection and technology transfer, including the possible removal of IPRs from multilateral trade rules. This matter could be included in the discussion on WTO reform as part of the broader effort at structural reform, economic recovery, and fostering more equitable growth and development across the world. Principles on technology transfer along with supportive multilateral mechanisms were part of previous efforts in UNCTAD to develop a Code of Conduct on Technology Transfer. Revisiting those initiatives would seem timely as we enter a new technological era with the potential to widen inequities across the global economy.

Re-aligning the Trade and Investment Regime

Stricter enforcement of existing national disclosure and reporting requirements for large corporations, such as through a global competition observatory, could facilitate the task of systematic information gathering on the large variety of existing regulatory frameworks, as a first step toward coordinated international best-practice guidelines and policies, and toward monitoring global market concentration trends and patterns.

The massive carbon imbalances in the trading system discussed earlier in the chapter must also be reversed. Similar to regulatory actions in the banking communities, carbon taxes on fossil fuels must be negotiated upwards in a development-friendly manner, while fossil fuel subsidies should be ratcheted downward. If negotiation on wider carbon tariffs does proceed, it would best serve the interests of development and climate commitments by building in a redistributive mechanism that redirects new tariff revenue to ring-fenced financing for green transitions in developing countries. Any requirement on governments in the Global South must be contingent on more effective policies of green technology transfers and new sources of financing to avoid a catastrophic impact on development initiatives. Incentive-based approaches should also be considered, for example optional preference schemes that provide ring-fenced climate financing additional to overseas development assistance. Considering the fiscal pressures facing many developing countries, such an approach – expanded policy space, green technology transfers, and additional sources of financing – is a more coherent way to keep warming below 1.5°C than simply reducing tariffs on an arbitrary collection of goods and services.

Preserve the right to regulate

Once the idea of trade and foreign investment as ends in themselves is rejected, the case is opened for providing more space for industrial and social investment policies. Private markets and international corporations will not supply the public goods that are necessary for a healthy economy and society, and using government subsidies to boost profitability in the hope of attracting more investment into public–private partnerships has a demonstrable record of failure. Too often, trade "liberalization" has been a veil for wage cutting and deregulation, themselves forms of subsidy with a poor record of delivering successful outcomes. On the other hand, the importance of providing subsidies as an additional support for industry during a crisis has been widely recognized. Industrial subsidies – including financial support to specific industries, tax credits, rent rebates to small and medium enterprises, export subsidies, and debt forgiveness – are important policy instruments which will be needed by developing countries to provide additional support to their domestic producers during and after the Covid-19 pandemic. These subsidies would enable the rebuilding and upgrading of labor-intensive and export-oriented industries, such as textiles and clothing, which have been hit hard in the South. Arrangements for managing subsidies rather than simply disciplining them will be needed in support of more resilient and sustainable outcomes.

Economics has shown time and again that incorporating the costs of financial crises, climate change, health-care, and worker protections makes economies more efficient and better off, not worse. Accordingly, governments need the flexibility and policy space to design and calibrate their integration into the global economy in terms of national economic priorities, and to boost social welfare. Powerful global firms have sought the deregulation of global markets as a form of implicit subsidy in their pursuit of more and more profit, while externalizing the costs of their actions on to households and the environment.

The governance of trade needs to be inclusive and transparent. The privatization of dispute resolution to private firms through the so-called Investor–State Dispute Settlement (ISDS) should be reversed. The WTO model of state-to-state dispute settlement, whereby nation states can properly weigh the private costs versus the social benefits, should be at the core of a multilateral trade system.

Make parallel investments, standards, and adjustment assistance

When the European Union became more economically integrated, it introduced a series of strong and uniform environment, health, and worker standards so that the lack of them could not become a source of competitiveness across Europe. Recognizing that some countries would have a difficulty in meeting those standards, the EU also set up adjustment funds for regions and individuals. The EU's mammoth European Investment Bank, along with national development banks such as Germany's KfW, were recapitalized to invest in the technologies and companies of the future to get them ready for the global marketplace. While many Europeans rightly criticize such efforts for not going far enough, their general approach and understanding are correct and need to be scaled up in Europe and built from the ground up across the world. The ratcheting up of tariffs on carbon and shifting subsidies from fossil fuels to clean energy would create incentives and mobilize massive resources for a just transition. Cracking down on misinvoicing tariffs would also create another huge pool of financing that – channeled through development banks – could help finance transitions and support the adjustment process as part of a global reform effort.

5

Catalyzing Development Finance

Alongside the need to provide a stable international monetary system and steer private capital flows away from speculative asset positions, increased long-term finance is critical to meeting development goals. In this regard, revitalizing public finance will be fundamental to rebuilding the world economy through a just transition to a zero-carbon global economy (UNCTAD 2019), just as it was for the policy-makers at Bretton Woods when they committed to a public finance model for the reconstruction of war-torn Europe and beyond. This was the task of the International Bank for Reconstruction and Development, better known today as the World Bank, as well as for the Marshall Plan, which took over the reconstruction effort. Other multilateral development banks (MDBs) were established at the regional level, such as the Asian Development Bank, the European Investment Bank, and others. There are now forty-five MDBs with just over $2 trillion in assets in total, the largest being the World Bank and its regional counterparts.

As discussed in Chapter 2 the idea of a publicly funded body dedicated to international financing by providing long-term capital was entirely novel. In his presentation to the House Banking Committee, Morgenthau (1945) was clear about its potential to free weaker countries "from the danger of economic aggression by more powerful neighbors."

Alongside the Western-led multilateral institutions, hundreds of national and regional development finance institutions (DFIs) have since emerged across the developing world. Today, there are over 450 of these institutions, with total assets of $11.6 trillion which may finance upwards of $2 trillion on an annual basis, representing roughly 12 percent of total world investment (Xu et al. 2020). Table 5.1 shows the top twenty-five DFIs in the world economy by total assets. Just these twenty-five represent 78 percent of the total assets of all DFIs. The World Bank is the seventh-largest DFI, while three of China's DFIs – the China Development Bank, the Agricultural Development Bank of China, and the Export-Import Bank of China – are in the top five. Indeed, these three China banks account for 34 percent of DFI assets globally. The European Investment Bank is the largest multilateral development bank. Germany, Italy, Brazil, and South Korea all have large DFIs as well.

Yet the current DFI regime suffers from three limitations. First, DFIs lack the scale and geographic coverage needed to play a catalyzing role in financing and providing adjustment assistance for a just transition to a zero-carbon economy. Second, much of the system remains misaligned with broader climate and development goals in terms of its policy toolkit. Third, much of the system lacks strong governance, and until very recently there has been a major lack of global coordination.

What is needed is a bold reform agenda to scale up public development finance on condition that it is aligned with a set of core principles around equality and sustainable development; that it helps finance the "adjustment" that will need to take place in the transition from a fossil-fuel-based society to a greener world; that it undertakes governance reform that gives more say to borrowers and affected communities; and that it embraces the wider network of development finance institutions that are not dominated by the advanced economies.

The Re-emergence of Development Finance

Public banks can be traced back to the nineteenth-century industrial revolution, especially in the later-arrival countries such as France and Germany, where the transition from an agrarian to an industrial economy was more capital-intensive than it had been in the first generation of European industrializers. Public banking gained further prominence in the immediate post-World War Two period, with reconstruction efforts in Germany (KfW), Japan (the Japan Development Bank), Brazil (BNDES), and South Korea (the Korean Development Bank). Gerschenkron (1962) provided a seminal discussion of the importance of these institutions in generating the investment required for late-industrializing economies to "catch up" in an environment where traditional sources of (individual or institutional) savings could not be adequately channeled by commercial intermediaries. There are clear parallels to the present moment, where public development finance will be crucial to ensuring that the world economy undergoes another transition.

Public banking, whether at the national, regional or international level, is clearly different in nature and orientation from private banking. Compared with private banking, there is, first, typically a focus on projects for which the social and/or developmental benefits exceed the purely commercial returns; on projects with long or uncertain lead times; on sectors or locations avoided by private finance; and on small borrowers who may lack collateral or a credit history. Second, the expectation is that loans will be offered under more favorable conditions than those of private or commercial banks, reflecting the initial government seed funding and public mandate. Third, costs are usually recovered, but not necessarily or always to their full extent, and repayments may occur over a longer time period. Some banks are expected to make a profit while others are not. But compared to private banks, profit is never supposed to be the sole measure of success.

These expectations and pressures are why public banks need a sufficiently large initial capitalization from government and reliable and stable sources of funds over time, whether from national treasury resources, debt securities, or pension funds. Many have to engage in a difficult balancing act, making profits on some projects and accepting losses on others, so that, on average, costs are sufficiently recovered and the bank can remain viable.

For the purposes of this book we rely on the conventional definition of development finance institutions as "government-sponsored financial

Figure 5.1 Number of newly established PDBs and DFIs

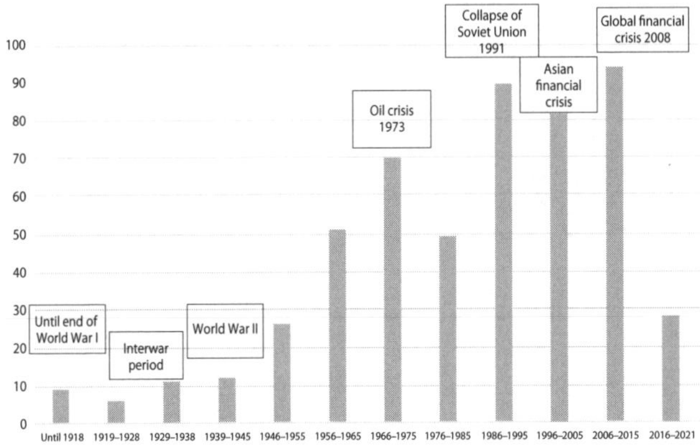

Source: Jiajun Xu, Regis Marodon, and Xinshun Ru, Qualifying and Identifying Public Development Banks and Development Financing Institutions, New Structural Economics Development Financing Research Report No. 2, November 2021.

institutions with the official mission to orient their operations to pursue public policy objectives" (Xu et al. 2020: 8). Figure 5.1 shows the net increase in DFIs over time, which has been steadily rising and saw a big uptick following the global financial crisis of 2008–9.

The turn of the century saw a renewal of interest in, and the increased relevance of, MDBs, for at least three reasons. First, there is increasing evidence that recent successful development experiences (South Korea, China) had a lot to do with the existence and expansion of public finance intermediaries. Second,

Table 5.1 25 Largest DFIs in the World Economy

Country/region	Bank	Acronym	Assets (Mls USD)
China	China Development Bank	CDB	2,352,293
China	Agricultural Development Bank of China	ADBC	996,287
Europe	European Investment Bank	EIB	636,687
China	Export–Import Bank of China	ChinaExim	609,695
Germany	Kreditanstalt für Wiederaufbau (KfW)	KfW	560,899
Italy	Cassa de Depositi y Prestiti	CDP	486,953
World	The World Bank	WB	403,056
Brazil	Caixa Econômica Federal	CAIXA	325,863
Canada	Caisse de dépôts et placement du Québec	CDPQ	256,518
Korea	Korea Development Bank	KDB	233,562
Brazil	Banco Nacional de Desenvolvimento Econômico e Social	BNDES	206,787
World	International Development Agency – WB group	IDA	201,591
Japan	Japan Finance Corporation	JFC	192,210
Asia	Asian Development Bank	AsDB	191,860
France	Caisse des dépôts et consignations	CDC	186,727
Germany	Development Bank of Hessen-Thuringia	HELABA	186,688
Germany	North Rhine–Westphalia Development Bank	NRWBank	170,801
Japan	Japan Bank for International Cooperation	JBIC	164,172

Netherlands	BNG Bank Nederlandse Gemeenten	BNG	157,523
Japan	Development Bank of Japan	DBJ	154,512
Saudi Arabia	National Development Fund of Saudi Arabia	NDFSA	130,000
Latin America/ Caribbean	Inter-American Development Bank	IADB	129,459
Japan	Japan International Cooperation Agency	JICA	111,917
		Top 25	9,046,060
		Percent of DFIs	78%

the commodity boom from 2003 to 2013 increased the reserve assets of many developing countries. These countries sought to recapitalize the MDBs but were only successful in doing so at the margins because of resistance from the advanced economies. Finally, following a series of international conferences in 2015, there has been a renewed ambition to achieve a number of interconnected global climate and development goals, and a recognition that commercial intermediaries are not up to the task.

The Limits of the Global DFI Regime

Taken as a whole, the current "system" of DFIs lacks the scale, effectiveness, and coordination necessary to support the rapid transformations that are needed in the world economy. Important steps have been taken in the right direction over the past half-decade, but they need to be scaled and accelerated. This section of the chapter will focus briefly on these three main limitations of the system: the lack of scale and coverage, the lack of an effective policy mix, and the lack of good governance and global coordination.

Lack of scale and coverage

Trillions of dollars need to be mobilized over the next decade to shift toward a green global economy in a just and inclusive manner, and DFIs are not scaled to that purpose. To achieve baseline SDGs and the upper bound of the Paris Agreement targets of 2°C (no estimates exist for the more desirable goal of 1.5°C), the global community will need to invest upwards of 7.6 percent of GDP on an annual basis to 2030. Current investment trends are estimated to amount to 5.5 percent of global GDP. We thus face a gap of at least 2.1 percent (Bhattacharya et al. 2019). According to research that screens development finance relative to the SDGs and climate goals, MDBs, national DFIs, and private capital flows are collectively covering only 2 percent of the global need, and 7.4 percent of the needs of emerging-market and developing countries. The largest providers of such investment are national DFIs, followed by private capital flows, and only then by the MDBs (Bhattacharya et al. 2019).

The private sector and national governments are doing little to address these gaps in long-run financing. Private capital flows are immense in scale but have proven to be biased toward short-term gains – flowing in "surges" and unstable "sudden stops" to emerging-market and developing countries – rather than long-term needs in infrastructure and human capital formation (see Chapter 3). Private-sector levels of investment in gross fixed capital formation have been on the decline in most countries for decades. In 1980 private-sector investment was over 20 percent of GDP, but has now declined to roughly 18 percent. As discussed in Chapter 3, there is an imperative for regulations that will align the financial system with climate and development goals.

DFIs, especially the World Bank and other Western-led institutions, have been using their balance sheets as a tool to mobilize the private sector, but have done so with little success. Their chosen route to crowd in the private sector is through numerous "de-risking" techniques and "blended finance" vehicles where MDBs agree to take on the riskier parts of projects so that the private sector is more comfortable committing the bulk of resources (and obtaining the subsequent financial rewards). However, after a decade of such efforts, the total spent on infrastructure projects with private participation decreased from a little over $150 billion in 2012 to less than $100 billion in 2019 (World Bank 2020).

The Global Infrastructure Facility, supported by the G20 and the World Bank for public-private partnerships (PPPs), has attracted a mere $45 billion in private investment and approved just $57.9 million after four years of existence. Of the limited resource mobilization that has occurred, it is not clear that it has been pro-poor, enhanced debt sustainability, or embraced broader development goals. According to the OECD, development finance institutions have mobilized just $81 billion toward the SDGs through blended finance since 2000 (OECD 2018). The majority of that financing has gone to developed and large middle-income countries. Only twenty-four of the poorest countries had a single infrastructure project with private participation between 2011 and 2015 (Humphrey 2018). The Inter-Agency Task Force on Financing for Development found that of the close to $50 billion mobilized by MDBs in private co-financing in 2016, only $1 billion flowed to the least developed countries, and there was little evidence that the most vulnerable in those countries were beneficiaries (Inter-Agency Task Force 2018: 92).

Poor development performance, but signs of change

The evidence on DFIs and economic growth is mixed. Bazzi and colleagues (2012) assessed the literature on the subject of MDBs and conducted their own statistical analysis to conclude that, by and large, DFIs "are systematically associated with modest, positive, subsequent growth." Recent work by Dreher and co-authors (2021) compared Chinese overseas development finance with that of the World Bank and found that while each Chinese-financed project had yielded a 0.41 to 1.49 percentage point increase in economic growth, there was no robust evidence that World Bank projects had promoted economic growth. That said, while average growth increases are important, growth has been unstable and its structure has not been conducive to long-run development, with many countries locked into an extractive growth path or debt-dependent consumption. Not all DFI finance is counter-cyclical either. Galindo and Panizza (2018) have confirmed that (as discussed in Chapter 3) private-sector flows are inherently pro-cyclical and that in general the MDBs are counter-cyclical in their financing – with the exception of banks in Africa and Europe. Evidence across the more than 400 national-level DFIs is more mixed, however. Griffith-Jones and Ocampo (2018) note the strong counter-cyclical tendencies of most DFIs in recent decades.

The MDBs and Western-led DFIs notoriously fostered financial instability in developing countries by providing them with large foreign-currency loans when they lacked the instruments to monitor debt sustainability and the government capacity to manage the finance and the projects themselves. What is more, the MDBs' "structural adjustment" programs designed to mitigate the damage caused by financial crises have often postponed development prospects by making new finance conditional on liberalization, deregulation, and privatization that lead to further instability and inequities (UNCTAD 1989; Rodrik 2011).

The record of DFIs on the environment and human rights is also checkered, to say the least. DFIs, both global and national, play a major role in financing big infrastructure and energy projects worldwide, and have thus essentially laid the foundation for the carbon-intensive patterns of economic growth across the world economy. Indeed, the world's current infrastructure investments account for the majority of carbon emissions globally (Davis et al. 2010). Despite the fact that many DFIs are shifting their balance sheets toward cleaner production, they are caught in a "hypocrisy trap" given that as recently as 2018 the largest DFIs were still steering less than a third of their investments into sustainable projects (Bhattacharya et al. 2019). While many of the Western-backed MDBs have shifted away from carbon-intensive investment, East Asian development banks operating globally have picked up the tab and their investments are now among the most carbon-intensive in the world (Chen et al. 2020). These investments have often also locked countries into extractive patterns of development that generate little employment, while their impacts on locally affected communities have been largely ignored. What is more, until recently, the gender and racial impacts of DFI activity have largely been ignored as well (Fox and Brown 1998; BWP 2019).

There has, however, been a recent shift on climate financing in many DFIs, including pledges to provide disincentives for economic activity that accentuates climate change, while simultaneously encouraging climate-friendly investments. Far and away the leader in this respect is the European Investment Bank, which has pledged to no longer finance coal in any form, upstream oil and gas extraction, or airport expansion, and to shift half of its balance sheet toward climate action by 2025. Many MDBs have introduced strict limits on the financing of coal-fired power plants, and the World Bank has pledged to end financing for upstream oil and gas extraction. Since 2018 the Inter-American Development Bank has screened all its projects for relevant climate risks, while the Caribbean Development Bank has explored the possibility of "climate-stress testing" its entire balance sheet to protect it from climate-related stranded assets (Monasterolo and Battiston 2016). Brazil's national development bank and the Development Bank of Southern Africa have created special climate funds, while the World Bank and the China Development Bank have been active in green bond markets, with the latter issuing a recent $500 million bond certified by the Climate Bond Initiative for low-carbon wind, transport, and water projects in China and Pakistan.

Lack of good governance and coordination

Part of the reason why DFIs have such a mixed record is due to poor governance. As in the case of the IMF, the global and Western-backed MDBs include no voice or representation for developing countries or the communities affected by their projects. The MDBs operate with a quota-based voting system similar to the IMF, giving the United States, Western Europe, and Japan the largest voting rights in many cases. Furthermore, as mentioned earlier, the president of the World Bank has always been a hand-picked citizen of the United States, and some previous presidents have embroiled the World Bank in corruption scandals (Parker 2009).

National-level DFIs can also have governance problems. Given their nature they do not have multilateral board structures, but research has shown that they can fall prey to rent-seeking behavior by recipients, and be used for political means in relation to development aims in some cases (Musacchio and Lazzerini 2014).

Finally, unlike the discussions around a global financial safety net, the network of DFIs hardly works as a "system" for setting joint goals and attempting to coordinate global action. Traditionally, the World Bank and the Western-backed MDBs meet twice a year in Washington, or occasionally in another location. They coordinate very tightly and there is a high degree of ideological conformity and harmonization across their policies. Until recently, most national and non-Western multilateral DFIs were highly fragmented across the world. In 2010 the International Development Finance Club (IDFC) was formed as a consortium of national and subregional DFIs. Being more than twice the size of the Western-backed MDBs, the IDFC can play a key role in delivering on a global just transition. In its first decade it began to coordinate on climate change and development finance (Morris 2018). The IDFC secretariat recently moved to the French Development Agency, which used the IDFC platform to host the first global "Finance in Common Summit," where all of the DFIs on the planet assembled to discuss joint goals and coordination.

Catalyzing Development Finance

A Reform Agenda

The world community needs to mobilize trillions of dollars annually in order to trigger a radical transformation of the world economy toward climate, health, and development goals. The private sector and national governments are falling far short of leading the way to financing these goals. In response, a G20 Eminent Persons Report on Global Financial Governance has sketched out a new "cooperative international order" tasked with unlocking the private capital needed to finance the big challenges of the twenty-first century. The key, the report suggests, is "de-risking" private investment and maximizing the contribution of development partners by joining up regional and global "platforms" to boost investment, primarily by creating new large-scale asset classes, such as "infrastructure assets," that can be "securitized" by bundling high- and low-risk loans into new and "safer" financial products. A focus on de-risking will, it is suggested, give international financial institutions greater scope to use public resources to incentivize private finance to invest in public goods and the global commons – for example through public guarantees, insurance programs, and co-investments. The report argues that the sense of urgency that now exists around the delivery of the SDGs could provide the impetus needed to scale up these innovations as part of a wider program to foster open, liquid capital markets that would help create investment opportunities.

Pursuing this approach to refashioning the multilateral financial system begs an obvious question: why, having crashed spectacularly in 2008–9, should this model be the preferred way to deliver on the ambition of the 2030 Agenda? The obvious answer is, it won't deliver. Indeed, a big part of the problem with the current system lies in governments already ceding far too much of a leadership role to private finance when it comes to meeting the SDG goals.

Global public policy challenges should be backed up with global public resources. DFIs are uniquely poised to provide and mobilize capital, but the effort to date has been undercapitalized, poorly governed, and uncoordinated. A reform agenda for each of these three shortcomings will require a major scaling up of resources on condition that governance and policy are aligned toward transitioning the global economy away from fossil fuels in a just and equitable manner. Doing so will mean facing up to recurrent governance matters with respect to policy space, leadership, and political economy. We will suggest in this chapter that one of the last gasps of the international New Dealers, the Marshall Plan, can offer some guidance for improving the governance of development finance in line with the global challenges of the twenty-first century.

Scale Up Development Finance

DFIs, especially the MDBs, will need a stepwise expansion and optimization of capital to meet common development goals. This can be accomplished by increasing the base capital of DFIs, expanding their lending headroom, and mobilizing capital from the commercial sector. Since the global financial crisis, some DFIs have made significant increases to the amount of DFI capital in the world economy, but a stepwise increase from these levels is still needed. Leading contributions have come from China, which has increased the assets of the China Development Bank by $1.5 trillion since the crisis, with roughly one-fifth of its balance sheet now in overseas financing to sovereign governments outside China. What is more, China has helped establish two new MDBs: the Asian Infrastructure Investment Bank and the New Development Bank. Many national and subregional development banks in emerging-market and developing countries also replenished DFIs or created new ones as they accumulated reserves due to the commodity boom in the aftermath of the crisis.

In addition to further capital increases, some DFIs have significant "lending headroom" to provide more financing while continuing to maintain strong credit ratings. A number of recent studies, including by rating agencies themselves, have estimated that MDBs could increase their lending headroom by $598 billion to $1.9 trillion under various scenarios. Without a capital increase, if MDBs optimized their balance sheets at an AAA rating, the increase ranges from $598 billion to $1 trillion. With a capital increase of 25 percent by major MDBs, lending could expand by $1.2 to $1.7 trillion. If some MDBs were to optimize at an AA+ rating, expansion could reach close to $2 trillion dollars. Optimizing at AA+ would, however, have a negative impact on profitability, though according to some the net benefits are still likely to be positive (Humphrey 2018; Munir and Gallagher 2020). In addition to expanding their lending headroom, some DFIs are considering securitizing their loan portfolios, though there are few examples of DFI securitization and estimates of the benefits and costs of such an approach are mixed at best (Humphrey 2018; Gabor 2019).

Aligning DFIs with Shared Goals

New financing for DFIs should be conditioned on their alignment with our broader goals and ambitions. What is more, DFIs will need to deploy new measurement and monitoring systems to ensure they maximize the development impacts and mitigate the development and financial risks of their efforts. They will have to phase out financing for fossil fuels and finance a just and green structural transformation across the world. New finance will need to go into massive green industrialization and employment efforts, and there will need to be significant adjustment financing for those in fossil-fuel-intensive industries.

A more effective network of public banking institutions at all levels will be needed to meet climate and development goals fairly and consistently. Such a network has already been proposed for the United States, modeled on the Reconstruction Finance Corporation of the New Deal era. By the time the RFC was officially dissolved in 1957, it was "among the largest and undoubtedly the most complex of all Federal lending agencies" (US Secretary of the Treasury 1959: v). It grew from small beginnings (with a capital of just $500 million paid in by the Treasury, and the right to leverage up to three times its equity) to create tens of billions of dollars of lending for the Depression-era reconstruction programs. It first issued bonds of $1.5 billion, using the borrowed moneys to pay for roads, bridges, dams, universities, and much more. In subsequent years it created loans for the US war effort and eventually for American business. Proceeds from the loans repaid the bonds. By the time the RFC was wound up, it had borrowed a total of $54 billion and made a net profit, as well as repaying most of the initial capitalization and generating income. The World Bank could be remodeled along these lines to play a pivotal role in the fight against climate change.

Key to measuring any monitoring progress is the need to increase transparency for measurement, evaluation, and accountability. Strengthened and improved Environmental and Social Risk Management (ESRM) systems beyond those that examine climate change will be essential to ensuring that development financing is calibrated toward broader goals. While most development banks deploy ESRM systems, their degree of effectiveness varies widely. Especially in the case of MDBs, ESRM has been perceived by host country finance ministries and by MDB operations staff as introducing onerous conditionalities that slow down project approval and completion without necessarily improving social and environmental outcomes. Research has shown that, when designed properly, safeguards such as environmental impact assessments, grievance mechanisms, and "free prior informed consent" by local communities can help DFIs identify and mitigate risks and improve project outcomes (Buntaine 2016).

Development finance institutions need to play a much bigger role in financing not only the transition but also the adjustment to it. Some firms, workers, fiscal systems, and financial markets are inherently tied to the fossil fuel industry. For example, South Africa's exposure to coal mining and coal-fired power plants as a source of foreign exchange and fiscal revenue, as a fuel for domestic power generation, and as a major, well-unionized, and racially diverse employer, presents a significant "transition risk" that is not unique (Huxman et al. 2019). Abandoning these sectors without adjustment will wreak havoc on livelihoods and on the fiscal and financial system. Economists estimate that the cost of a "just transition transaction" for South Africa that safeguards workers and the financial system while shifting from coal to clean power would be around $11 billion (Winkler et al. 2020).

The Case for a New Bretton Woods

Global Cooperation and Governance

Without the proper governance the revitalization of global development finance will not be effective or just. This is all the more urgent as the hegemonic role of the United States, while not over, is certainly weakening. "A vision of a system serving all developing countries requires a governance structure that permits adequate voice" (Bhattacharya et al. 2018: 6). Aligning national development banks, borrower-led subregional DFIs, and the MDBs, as well as reaching out to wider civil society participation, would provide for a more cohesive and legitimate system to coordinate and calibrate global DFI financing toward our common future. The global MDBs, like the IMF, need quota-based increases in order to expand not only the scale of the institutions but also their voice and representation. What is more, MDBs need merit-based leaders rather than those picked by nationality (EPG 2018). National-level banks and MDBs alike need performance requirements and accountability mechanisms that ensure finance is calibrated to climate and development goals.

Rather than an elite Western-led coordination through the World Bank, the concept of the "Finance in Common" summit should be built on but expanded in terms of instrumentation and stakeholder engagement. There are limitless opportunities and agendas for a global forum of coordination and cooperation across DFIs. Shared country strategies, the development of regional approaches (especially for infrastructure), and dialogue on safeguards and standards could all be part of such an agenda. Over time some of the best practices discussed above could be scaled up. Proposals for such cooperation include a global special-purpose vehicle and global guarantee funds for sustainable infrastructure, and the creation of project platforms to facilitate crowding-in private investment, among others (Lee 2018; Studart and Gallagher 2018).

A more ambitious approach to scaling up and coordinating a just transition could follow the example of the Marshall Plan. The Plan is often invoked by politicians for its ambitious tackling of a big problem with bold solutions. But much of this discussion takes place with little or no appreciation of the original design (Kozul-Wright and Rayment 2007). While historians continue to debate the role and impact of the Plan on post-war European reconstruction, it offers some key "how-to" lessons that resonate with today's crisis.

First, Marshall-style planning can't be done on the cheap. In rolling out the Plan, the United States committed over 1 percent of its national income each year over a four-year period. Second, it can't be done under the deadweight of debt. Marshall aid consisted largely of grants, on the clear recognition that heavy debt-servicing obligations would hold back the investment needed for recovery and longer-term growth. Third, it can't be advanced through piecemeal assistance or by imposing solutions on a devastated population. Respecting national sensibilities and preferences as well as drawing on local knowledge and expertise were key ingredients of the Plan's success.

These lessons are particularly important when thinking about the combined climate, health, and development challenges behind any meaningful recovery plan that must move quickly from delivering relief to building resilience, particularly in the developing world. The United Nations and the G20 have sketched out the elements needed to meet the immediate health emergency in the developing world, but if the mission is, as it should be, to ensure resilience to future health shocks, relief cannot be separated from related policy challenges around sanitation, food security, precarious work, and housing conditions.

So what could an updated Marshall Plan look like? First, talk of international solidarity must carry matching financial commitments. If the generosity of the United States more than seventy years ago is too high a target, it should not be too much to expect the donor community to finally meet the 0.7% Official Development Assistance (ODA) target for the next two years. Doing so would generate something in the order of $380 billion above current commitments. An additional $220 billion mobilized by the network of multilateral and regional financing institutions could complete a $600 billion support package within eighteen to twenty months. This would require a boost to their capital base, made possible through transfers from the bank's shareholders, augmented by borrowing on international capital markets, with a measured relaxing of their fidelity to financial sobriety.

Second, the money should be dispersed largely as grants but with some room for zero-interest loans, the precise mixture determined as the emergency response evolves. The looming developing-country debt crisis will have to be dealt with through complementary actions, including an immediate standstill on debt payments followed by restructuring and cancellation.

Finally, given its multifaceted nature, the recovery effort will require a dedicated agency, drawing, like the Marshall Plan, on the personnel of existing agencies as well as from the private sector, with local expertise and coordination involved from the outset. A central financing and oversight agency linked to national public agencies through a regional coordination mechanism, much like in the original Plan, remains a model to follow.

Having a remodeled World Bank play that role along the lines of the RFC, as suggested above, would be one option. Former IMF chief economist Ken Rogoff has instead proposed a global carbon bank as an alternative, on the grounds that we need a dedicated institution that is not encumbered with multiple goals (Rogoff 2019). However, that would seem to diminish the interrelated nature of the challenges the world is now facing. A bolder option would be to go back to one of the original ideas of the international New Dealers and fashion such an institution on the Tennessee Valley Authority (Helleiner 2014). This combined an infusion of public capital with a network of public institutions to advance an integrated policy program and construct related physical infrastructure in support of a transformation of the economy of the southern United States, whilst also building broad-based local support for its programs.

6

Crises, Reform, and Countervailing Power

People everywhere desire much the same things: a decent job, a secure home, a safe environment, a better future for their children, and a government that listens and responds to their concerns. In truth, they want a different deal from that offered by the sirens of free trade and footloose capital. A new deal for people and the planet must respond to these needs and aspirations. It will begin at the level of local communities but it will be grounded at the national level in effective public policy, representative institutions, and strong regulatory structures. However, in today's interdependent and uneven world, any hope of achieving a just transition to an inclusive and sustainable future will have to confront the global forces that constrain the ambitions of a Green New Deal. The support of an effective multilateral order will be crucial.

The Case for a New Bretton Woods

We have argued in this volume that the current order does not pass muster, in large part because the economic interests that dominate our hyper-globalized world have rigged the rules of the international economy in favor of the privileged few (both within and across countries), stifling democratic voice in the process, and draining trust from the institutions of international governance.

The multilateral institutions established during and immediately after World War Two are still operational, but they have lost their connection to the guiding principles laid out by Henry Morgenthau, Roosevelt's Treasury Secretary and the host at Bretton Woods, in his address to the US Congress (see Chapter 2). Instead, they have in recent decades pursued an agenda which encourages footloose capital, bolsters (and protects) private profit, and reduces the policy space available to governments. As a result, they have acted as handmaidens to an age of rising inequality and heightened anxiety.

The required reset of the international system to face the contemporary economic and environmental challenges will not succeed through backroom diplomacy and grand summitry. As was the case in the 1930s and 1940s, new coalitions are needed, at the global as well as the national level, to mobilize against the powerful vested interests that have woven strong political alliances around support for footloose capital, rent-seeking corporations, and a carbonized economy (Blyth and Oatley 2021).

The alternative lies with a global Green New Deal built around a strong public investment drive to decarbonize contemporary life, and a just transition that can deliver changes on the regulatory, redistribution, and resilience fronts designed to make tangible improvements in the lives of the majority of people, particularly in the developing world. While the Covid-19 crisis has served as a reminder of just how unprepared most governments are in the face of large-scale shocks, it has also helped to revive critical components of this alternative strategy that have been buried under the ideological wreckage left by four decades of market fundamentalism.

The crisis has, first and foremost, forced us to think again about solidarity, common purpose, and the essential components of a healthy and resilient society. The idea of a social contract has returned to political discussions, with the *Financial Times* an unexpected champion, drawing equally unexpected policy conclusions: "Radical reforms – reversing the prevailing policy direction of the last four decades – will need to be put on the table. Governments will have to accept a more active role in the economy. They must see public services as investments rather than liabilities, and look for ways to make labour markets less insecure. Redistribution will again be on the agenda; the privileges of the elderly and wealthy in question" (April 3, 2020).

Rethinking the role of government is a second consequence of the crisis. Talk of the active state has become commonplace, but a more useful concept, and not just for developing countries, is that of the developmental state (Chang 1999). Whilst a vast literature has grown up around the concept, its focus has been on the key role of the state in the process of capital formation, both through its own (public) investment strategy and through its capacities to coordinate, incentivize, and discipline private investors. The lessons from developmental states that have been successful in mobilizing resources for large-scale investment drives are certainly germane to the challenges around a just transition (Gabor 2021). Moreover, in one way or another – and which way does matter – industrial policy is back on the agenda (Pollin 2020).

The last concept to make a comeback is that of countervailing power. This was coined by the economist John Kenneth Galbraith (1952) in his assessment of post-World War Two capitalism in the United States, but its political roots lie in Roosevelt's call to labor and civil rights activists to help him implement bold legislation. Much of the post-war discussion centered on the concentration and accumulation of market power in the hands of large industrial firms, a concentration which threatened a squeeze on suppliers, consumers, and workers through unfair prices and wages. Galbraith argued that bargaining collectively with larger firms, through labor unions and civil society organizations, was the only way to counter their power, including, at the national level, by shaping legislation to reduce market concentration and rebalance economies.

Arguably, it is this concept of countervailing power which is most urgently in need of a contemporary makeover if the systemic crises of the twenty-first century are to be effectively addressed. In *This Changes Everything*, Naomi Klein celebrated the emergence of resistance movements armed with economic alternatives for ways of living within planetary boundaries (Klein 2014). Without diminishing the devastation arising from financial crises, heightened inequality, and climate destruction, Klein argued that things would have been much worse if not for the countervailing pressure of these movements in pushing back against corporate interests. Those movements have since grown stronger. Still, who is holding the levers of the state will be critical in determining what kind of coalitions are formed to rebalance the economy in support of people and the planet.

In the United States and across Europe, "Green New Deal" coalitions have emerged in the last five years that link concerns over equality and rights with green structural transformation. Policy-makers were taking note even before Covid-19, but talk of green recovery strategies is now commonplace. Central banks, having rediscovered the benefits of functional finance, are now pushing at the frontiers of climate finance. City and regional governments have moved in innovative, often bold, directions. Significantly, labor organizations have begun to acknowledge the opportunities that green jobs could provide to their members, and to link these to progressive possibilities in related sectors such as the care economy. International labor bodies such as the ITUC and Public Services International have made a just transition central to their organizing work. Much of this still remains inchoate and below scale, but the shared narrative and many of the policy details suggest an opportunity for building stronger and more intersectional ties within and across countries.

Developing countries have also been striving to strengthen their climate ambition as part of efforts to meet the Sustainable Development Goals. Argentina, Barbados, Pakistan, South Africa, South Korea, Uruguay, and Vietnam, to name just a few, all have initiatives that look to ground green new deals in their local circumstances. Many have already made big strides in shifting to renewable sources of energy. However, their lack of policy and fiscal space has been confirmed by the Covid-19 crisis, while the barriers posed by private creditors, intellectual-property owners, and tax-avoiding multinationals are posing additional obstacles to mobilizing finance and accessing technology in support of alternative development strategies.

Unlike in the 1970s, developing countries have not been able to build the kind of solidarity that pushed the idea of a new international economic order to the forefront of international negotiations. Still, emerging-market and developing countries have formed coalitions to galvanize countervailing power at international economic institutions, both at the WTO to block the advance of further neoliberal rules and build South–South coalitions to push for more development-friendly measures (Hopewell 2018), as well as at the IMF to push for more voice and representation and for a new "view" on capital controls (Gallagher 2015). The BRICS and others have also created a number of their own development banks, reserve funds, and trading areas that have better rules and governance. These institutions give developing countries more voice, but also provide healthy institutional competition and more leverage at the international institutions themselves (Grabel 2018; Gallagher 2015).

Hovering over these new initiatives and sources of leadership is the inevitable question of what role a hegemonic power could or should play in building a better future for all. It is a difficult question. As Varoufakis (2013) has noted, the attempts at hegemonic leadership over the past century have run afoul of the "paradox of success," whereby the very economic strength that enables the hegemon to play a leadership role tends eventually to undermine the self-restraint on which that leadership depends, eroding trust both within the hegemon itself and across the system. The inevitable result is a slide toward some kind of neo-mercantilist system instead.

The erosion of trust in the system has been complicated by the rise of China, whose economic success has made it an essential player in any global climate strategy. Despite operating in an international economic environment designed to advantage large corporations from advanced economies, China has employed considerable policy acumen to develop and diversify its own economy (Poon and Kozul-Wright 2019). This has not only propelled the fastest reduction in extreme poverty in human history, but also made China the largest single emitter of greenhouse gases in the global economy. China's transformation has also provoked an increasingly hostile stance from advanced economies. While that hostility is as much about their own profound policy failures as it is about the malfeasance of Chinese policy-makers – and it has, on a positive note, already triggered a race to the top in terms of climate targets and regulatory commitments – it is arguably the most serious obstacle to improving coordination and increasing cooperation among the key players, which is needed to ensure a multilateral system fit for purpose.

We need a Bretton Woods moment to align national goals and coalitions globally. Such a moment should not only be a Western one, and not closeted in a tiny New Hampshire town, but should form part of a global conversation that includes voices from Bali, Bogotá, Buenos Aires, Berlin, Biloxi, Brazzaville, Beijing, Bangalore, and beyond. Dr. King was right that there is such a thing as being too late, and in the case of the climate being too late will have catastrophic consequences across the planet. There is still time, but there is not time for apathy or complacency. This, as King would surely have recognized, "is a time for vigorous and positive action."

Bibliography

Abdelal, R. (2007). *Capital Rules: The Construction of Global Finance*. Cambridge, MA: Harvard University Press.

Acemoglu, D., D. Autor, D. Dorn, G. Hanson, and B. Price (2016). Import Competition and the Great US Employment Sag of the 2000s. *Journal of Labor Economics* 34(S1), Part 2.

Ackerman, F. and K. P. Gallagher (2008). The Shrinking Gains from Global Trade Liberalization in Computable General Equilibrium Models: A Critical Assessment. *International Journal of Political Economy* 37(1), 50–77.

Aizenman, J. and G. K. Pasricha (2010). Selective Swap Arrangements and the Global Financial Crisis: Analysis and Interpretation. *International Review of Economics & Finance* 19(3), 353–65.

Akyuz, Y. (2017). *Playing with Fire: Deepened Financial Integration and Changing Vulnerabilities of the Global South*. Oxford: Oxford University Press.

Altamura, E. (2017). The Paradox of the 1970s: The Renaissance of International Banking and the Rise of Public Debt. In Hartmut Berghoff and Laura Rischbieter (eds.), *Living on Easy Credit: Public Debt and Financialization in the Western World after 1945*, special issue, *Journal of Modern European History* 15(4), 489–502.

Amsden, A. (2001). *The Rise of the Rest: Challenges to the West from Late-Industrializing Economies*. Oxford: Oxford University Press.

Autor, D., D. Dorn, L. F. Katz, C. Patterson, and J. Van Reenen (2020). The Fall of the Labor Share and the Rise of the Superstar Firms. *Quarterly Journal of Economics* 135(2), 645–709.

Bazzi, S., R. Bhavnani, M. Clemens, and S. Radelet (2012). Counting Chickens When They Hatch: Timing and the Effects of Aid on Growth. *Economic Journal* 122, 590–617.

Bhattacharya, A. et al. (2018). *The New Global Agenda and the Future of the Multilateral Development Bank System*. Washington, DC: Brookings Institution.

Bhattacharya, A., K. P. Gallagher, M. Muñoz Cabré, M. Jeong, and X. Ma (2019). *Aligning G20 Infrastructure Investment with Climate Goals and the 2030 Agenda*. Foundations 20 Platform, a report to the G20.

Bibliography

Blyth, M. (2002). *Great Transformations: Economic Ideas and Institutional Change in the Twentieth Century*. Cambridge: Cambridge University Press.

Blyth, M. and T. Oatley (2021). The Death of the Carbon Coalition. *Foreign Policy*, February 12.

Boyce, R. (2009). *The Great Interwar Crisis and the Collapse of Globalization*. New York: Macmillan.

Bradford, S. C., P. L. E. Grieco, and G. G. Hufbauer (2005). *The Payoff to America from Global Integration*. Peterson Institute for International Economics.

Bradlow, D. D. and S. K. Park (2020). A Global Leviathan Emerges: The Federal Reserve, COVID-19, and International Law. *American Journal of International Law* 114(4), 657–65.

Bretton Woods Project (2019). What Are the Main Criticisms of the World Bank and the IMF? At https://www.brettonwoodsproject.org/2019/06/what-are-the-main-criticisms-of-the-world-bank-and-the-imf.

Buntaine, M. (2016). *Giving Aid Effectively: The Politics of Environmental Performance and Selectivity at Multilateral Development Banks*. Oxford: Oxford University Press.

Caliendo, L. and F. Parro (2015). Estimates of the Trade and Welfare Effects of NAFTA. *National Bureau of Economic Research* 82(1), 1–44.

Cambridge Centre for Risk Studies (2018). *Global Risk Index 2019 Executive Summary*. Cambridge Centre for Risk Studies, University of Cambridge.

Camdessus, M. (1997). Global Capital Flows: Raising the Returns and Reducing the Risks. Speech to Los Angeles World Affairs Council, 17 June.

Campiglio, E., Y. Dafermos, P. Monnin et al. (2018). Climate Change Challenges for Central Banks and Financial Regulators. *Nature Climate Change* 8, 462–8.

Carl, J. and D. Fedor (2016). Tracking Global Carbon Revenues: A Survey of Carbon Taxes versus Cap-and-Trade in the Real World. *Energy Policy* 96, 50–77.

Chang, H. (1999). The Economic Theory of the Developmental State. In M. Woo-Cumings, ed. *The Developmental State*. New York: Cornell University Press, pp. 182–99.

Chen, X., K. P. Gallagher, and D. L. Mauzerall (2020). Chinese Overseas Development Financing of Electric Power Generation: A Comparative Analysis. *One Earth* 3, 491–503.

Chwieroth, J. M. (2010). *Capital Ideas: The IMF and the Rise of Financial Liberalization*. Princeton: Princeton University Press.

Climate, Weather, and Catastrophe Insight (2021). Annual Report 2020, at http://thoughtleadership.aon.com/Documents/20210125-if-annual-cat-report.pdf.

Cooper, R. (1982). The Gold Standard: Historical Facts and Future Prospects. *Brookings Papers on Economic Activity* 13(1): 1–56.

Copelovitch, M. S. (2010). Master or Servant? Common

Bibliography

Agency and the Political Economy of IMF Lending. *International Studies Quarterly* 54(1), 49–77.

Dagah, H., W. Kring, and D. Bradlow (2019). Jump-Starting the African Monetary Fund. GEGI Policy Brief 008, Global Development Policy Center, Boston University.

Davies, R. (2019). The Politics of Trade in the Era of Hyperglobalization. *South Centre*. At https://www.southcentre.int/wp-content/uploads/2019/11/Bk_2019_The-Politics-of-Trade-in-the-Era-of-Hyperglobalisation-A-Southern-African-Perspective_EN.pdf.

Davies, R., R. Kozul-Wright, R. Banga, K. Gallogly-Swan, and J. Capaldo (2021). *Reforming the International Trading System for Recovery, Resilience, and Inclusive Development*. Geneva: UNCTAD.

Davis, S. J., K. Caldeira, and D. Matthews (2010). Future CO_2 Emissions and Climate Change from Existing Energy Infrastructure. *Science* 329(5997), 1330–3.

De Gregorio, D., B. E. Jose, T. Ito, and C. Wyplosz (2018). IMF Reform: The Unfinished Agenda. Geneva Reports on the World Economy, Geneva: International Center for Monetary and Banking Studies and the Centre for Economic Policy Research.

Dong He and R. McCauley (2010). Offshore Markets for the Domestic Currency: Monetary and Financial Stability Issues. BIS Working Papers 320, Bank for International Settlements.

Dreher, A., A. Fuchs, B. Parks, A. Strange, and M. Tierney

(2021). Aid, China, and Growth: Evidence from a New Global Development Finance Dataset. *American Economic Journal* 13(2), 135–74.

Dreher, A., J-E. Sturm, and J. R. Vreeland (2015). Politics and IMF Conditionality. *Journal of Conflict Resolution* 59(1), 120–48.

Eichengreen, B. (2008). *Globalizing Capital: A History of the International Monetary System*. Princeton: Princeton University Press.

Eichengreen, B. (2012). *Exorbitant Privilege: The Rise and Fall of the Dollar*. Oxford: Oxford University Press.

EPG (2018). Making the Global Financial System Work for All. G20 Eminent Persons Group, at https://www.globalfinancialgovernance.org/assets/pdf/G20EPG-Full%20Report.pdf.

Evenett, S. J. and M. Meier (2008). An Interim Assessment of the US Trade Policy of "Competitive Liberalization." *World Economy* 31(1), 31–66.

Felix, D. (1961). An Alternative View of the Monetarist–Structuralist Controversy. In A. Hirschman (ed.), *Latin American Issues: Essays and Comments*. New York: The Twentieth Century Fund.

Fox, J. and D. Brown (1998). *The Struggle for Accountability: The World Bank, NGOs and Grassroots Movements*. Cambridge, MA: MIT Press.

Furceri, D., P. Loungani, and J. D. Ostry (2019). The Aggregate and Distributional Effects of Financial

Globalization: Evidence from Macro and Sectoral Data. *Journal of Money, Credit and Banking* 53, 163–98.

Gabor, D. (2019). Securitization for Sustainability? Heinrich Boel Foundation, at https://us.boell.org/sites/default/files/gabor_finalized.pdf.

Gabor, D. (2021). The Wall Street Consensus. *Development and Change* 52(3), 429–59.

Galbraith, J. K. (1952). *American Capitalism: The Concept of Countervailing Power*. Boston: Houghton Mifflin.

Galindo, A. and U. Panizza (2018). The Cyclicality of International Public Sector Borrowing in Developing Countries: Does the Lender Matter? *World Development* 112, 119–35.

Gallagher, K. P. (2008a). Trading Away the Ladder? Trade Politics and Economic Development in the Americas. *New Political Economy* 13, 37–59.

Gallagher, K. P. (2008b). Understanding Developing Country Resistance to the Doha Round. *Review of International Political Economy* 15(1), 62–85.

Gallagher, K. P. (2013). *The Clash of Globalizations: Essays on Trade and Development Policy*. London: Anthem Press.

Gallagher, K. P. (2015). *Ruling Capital: Emerging Markets and the Reregulation of Cross-border Financial Flows*. Ithaca: Cornell University Press.

Gallagher, K. P., G. Lagarda, and J. Linares (2019).

Capital Openness and Income Inequality: Smooth Sailing or Troubled Waters? In Jose Antonio Ocampo (ed.), *International Policy Rules and Inequality: Implications for Global Economic Governance*. New York: Columbia University Press.

Gallagher, K. P., H. Gao, W. Kring, and U. Volz (2020). Safety First: Expanding the Global Financial Safety Net in Response to COVID-19. *Global Policy*, November.

Gallagher, K. S. (2006). *China Shifts Gears: Automakers, Oil, Pollution, and Development*. Cambridge, MA: MIT Press.

Gao, H. and K. P. Gallagher (2019). Strengthening the International Monetary Fund for Stability and Sustainable Development. T20 Task Force on International Finance, Japan. At https://www.g20-in sights.org/policy_briefs/strenthening-the-international -monetary-fund-for-stability-and-sustainable-develop ment.

Garcia, F. (2004). Beyond Special and Differential Treatment. *Boston College International and Comparative Law Review* 27, 291–317.

Georgieva, K. (2020). A New Bretton Woods Moment. Speech at the International Monetary Fund, October 15.

Gerschenkron, A. (1962). *Economic Backwardness in Historical Perspective*. Cambridge, MA: The Belknap Press of Harvard University Press.

Ghosh, A., J. Ostry, and M. Qureshi (2018). *Taming the*

Tide of Capital Flows: A Policy Guide. Cambridge, MA: MIT Press.

Grabel, I. (2018). *When Things Don't Fall Apart: Global Financial Governance and Developmental Finance in an Age of Productive Incoherence.* Cambridge, MA: MIT Press.

Graz, J. C. (2014). The Havana Charter: When State and Market Shake Hands. In E. Reinert, R. Kattel, and J. Ghosh (eds.), *Handbook of Alternative Theories of Economic Development.* Cheltenham: Edward Elgar.

Greenspan, A. (2005). Economic Flexibility. National Italian American Foundation, Washington, DC, October 12.

Griffith-Jones, S. and J. A. Ocampo (eds.) (2018). *The Future of National Development Banks.* Oxford: Oxford University Press.

Guzman, M. and Heymann, D. (2015). The IMF Debt Sustainability Analysis: Issues and Problems. *Journal of Globalization and Development* 6(2), 387–404.

Hanson, G. (2021). Can Trade Work for Workers? *Foreign Affairs*, May–June.

Helleiner, E. (1994). *States and the Re-emergence of Global Finance.* Ithaca: Cornell University Press.

Helleiner, E. (2014). *Forgotten Foundations of Bretton Woods International Development and the Making of the Postwar Order.* Ithaca: Cornell University Press.

Hirschman, A. (1945). *National Power and the Structure of Foreign Trade*. Berkeley: University of California Press.

Hopewell, K. (2018). *Breaking the WTO: How Emerging Powers Disrupted the Neoliberal Project*. Stanford: Stanford University Press.

Humphrey, C. (2018). Channeling Private Investment to Infrastructure: What Can MDBs Realistically Do? London: Overseas Development Institute, Working Paper 534.

Huxman, M., M. Answar, and D. Nelson (2019). *Understanding the Impact of a Low Carbon Transition on South Africa*. San Francisco: Climate Policy Initiative.

Ikenberry, J. G. (2020). *A World Safe for Democracy: Liberal Internationalism and the Crises of Global Order*. New Haven: Yale University Press.

IMF (2013). Energy Subsidy Reform: Lessons and Implications. At https://www.imf.org/en/Publications/Policy-Papers/Issues/2016/12/31/Energy-Subsidy-Reform-Lessons-and-Implications-PP4741.

IMF (2017). Adequacy of the Global Financial Safety Net. Considerations for Fund Toolkit Reform. IMF Policy Paper. Washington, DC: International Monetary Fund.

IMF (2018). Structural Conditionality in IMF-Supported Programs – Evaluation Update. Washington, DC: International Monetary Fund. At https://ieo.imf.org/

en/our-work/evaluation-reports/Updates/Structural-Conditionality-in-IMF-Supported-Programs-Eval.

IMF (2020). Articles of Agreement. At https://www.imf.org/external/pubs/ft/aa/index.htm.

Ingraham, C. and H. Schneider (2014). Industry Voices Dominate the Trade Advisory System. *Washington Post*, February 27.

Inter-Agency Task Force on Financing for Development (2018). *Financing for Development: Progress and Prospects 2018*. New York: United Nations.

Izurieta A., P. Kohler and J. Pizarro (2018). Financialization, Trade, and Investment Agreements: Through the Looking Glass or through the Realities of Income Distribution and Government Policy? GDAE/UNCTAD Working Paper 18–02.

James, H. (2001). *The End of Globalization: Lessons from the Great Depression*. Cambridge, MA: Harvard University Press.

Jeanne, O., A. Subramanian, and J. Williamson (2012). *Who Needs an Open Capital Account?* Washington, DC: Peterson Institute for International Economics.

Johnson, L., B. Skartvedt Güven, and J. Coleman (2017). Investor–State Dispute Settlement: What Are We Trying to Achieve? Does ISDS Get Us There? Privatizing Dispute Resolution. Columbia University, Columbia Center on Sustainable Investment. At https://ccsi.columbia.edu/news/investor-state-dispute-settlement-what-are-we-trying-achieve-does-isds-get-us-there.

Katznelson, I. (2013). *Fear Itself: The New Deal and the Origins of Our Times*. New York: W. W. Norton and Co.

Keen, S. (2017). *Can We Survive Another Financial Crisis?* London: Polity Press.

Kentikelenis, A., T. Stubbs, and L. King (2016). IMF Conditionality and Development Policy Space, 1985–2014. *Review of International Political Economy* 23(4), 534–82.

Keynes, J. M. (1980). Letter to Lord Addison, May 1944. In D. Moggridge (ed.), *The Collected Writings of John Maynard Keynes, Volume XXVI*. London: Macmillan.

Kindleberger, C. P. (1973). *The World in Depression, 1929–1939*. Berkeley: University of California Press.

King, M. L. (1967). Beyond Vietnam. Speech delivered by Dr. Martin Luther King, Jr., on April 4, 1967, at a meeting of Clergy and Laity Concerned at Riverside Church in New York City.

Klein, M. and M. Pettis (2020). *Trade Wars Are Class Wars: How Rising Inequality Distorts the Global Economy and Threatens International Peace*. New Haven: Yale University Press.

Klein, N. (2014). *This Changes Everything*. London: Penguin.

Korinek, A. and J. Kreamer (2014). The Redistributive Effects of Financial Deregulation. *Journal of Monetary Economics* 68, S55–S67.

Bibliography

Kozul-Wright, R. and P. Rayment (2007). *The Resistible Rise of Market Fundamentalism*. London: Zed.

Kring, W. and W. Grimes (2019). Leaving the Nest: The Rise of Regional Financial Arrangements and the Future of Global Governance. *Development and Change* 50(1), 72–95.

Kroeber, A. R. (2016). *China's Economy: What Everyone Needs to Know*. London: Oxford University Press.

Krueger, A. (2001). A New Approach to Sovereign Debt Restructuring. Washington, DC: IMF. At https://www.imf.org/en/News/Articles/2015/09/28/04/53/sp112601.

Kumhof, M., R. Rancière, and P. Winant (2013). Inequality, Leverage and Crisis: The Case of Endogenous Default. IMF Working Paper 249. Washington, DC: International Monetary Fund.

Kuttner, Robert (2018), Can Democracy Survive Capitalism? New York, Norton and Co.

Lamy, P. (2006). Humanizing Globalization. Speech, Santiago de Chile, Chile, January 30.

Lazonick, W., M. Erdem Sakinc, and M. Hopkins (2020). Why Stock Buybacks Are Dangerous for the Economy. *Harvard Business Review*, January 7.

Lee, N. (2018). *Billions to Trillions? Issues on the Role of Development Banks in Mobilizing Private Finance*. Washington, DC: Center for Global Development.

McKay, J., U. Volz, and R. Wölfinger (2011). Regional Financing Arrangements and the Stability of the International Monetary System. *Journal of Globalization and Development* 2(1), Article 1.

Martin, J. (2013). Were We Bullied? *London Review of Books*, November 21.

Mazower, M. (2013). *Governing the World: The History of an Idea*. London: Penguin Books.

Mehrling, P. (2015). Elasticity and Discipline in the Global Swap Network. *International Journal of Political Economy* 44(4), 311–24.

Mohan, R. and M. Kapur (2015). Emerging Powers and Global Economic Governance: Whither the IMF? Washington, DC: International Monetary Fund. At https://www.imf.org/external/pubs/ft/wp/2015/wp152 19.pdf.

Monasterolo, I. and S. Battiston (2016). Assessing Portfolios' Exposure to Climate Risks: An Application of the CLIMAFIN-tool to the Caribbean Development Bank's Projects Portfolio. Final Deliverable Technical Assistance for Climate Action Support to the Caribbean Development Bank TA2013036 R0 IF2.

Morgenthau, H. (1944). Closing Address. In Department of State (ed.), *United Nations Monetary and Financial Conference: Bretton Woods, Final Act and Related Documents, New Hampshire, July 1 to July 22, 1944*. Washington, DC: United States Government Printing Office.

Morgenthau, H. (1945). Statement of Secretary Morgenthau before the Committee on Banking and Currency of the House of Representatives (Washington, March 7, 1945). At https://www.cvce. eu/content/publication/2003/12/8/c31a8eb2-aaca-471 e-a29e-1e5eaba9bd2e/ publishable_en.pdf.

Morris, S. (2018). *The International Development Finance Club and the Sustainable Development Goals.* Washington, DC: Center for Global Development.

Moschella, M. (2012). IMF Surveillance in Crisis: The Past, Present and Future of the Reform Process. *Global Society* 26(1), 43–60.

Munir, W. and K. P. Gallagher (2020). Scaling Up for Sustainable Development: Benefits and Costs of Expanding and Optimizing Balance Sheets in the Multilateral Development Banks. *Journal of International Development* 32, 222–43.

Musacchio, A. and S. Lazzarini (2014). *Reinventing State Capitalism.* Cambridge, MA: Harvard University Press.

Narlikar, A. (2004). Developing Countries and the WTO. In B. Hocking and S. McGuire (eds.), *Trade Politics: International, Domestic, and Regional Perspectives*, 2nd edition. London: Routledge.

Norfield, T. (2016). *The City: London and the Global Power of Finance.* London: Verso.

Ocampo, J. A. (2018). *Resetting the International Monetary (Non)System.* Oxford: Oxford University Press.

OECD (2018). *Making Blended Finance Work for the Sustainable Development Goals*. Paris: OECD.

Ortiz, I. (2018). The Case for Universal Social Protection. *Finance & Development* 55(4). At https://www.imf .org/external/pubs/ft/fandd/2018/12/case-for-univers al-social-protection-ortiz.htm.

Ostry, J. D. et al. (2010). Capital Inflows: The Role of Control. At https://www.imf.org/external/pubs/ft/ spn/2010/spn1004.pdf.

Ostry, J. D. et al. (2012). Multilateral Aspects of Managing the Capital Account. IMF Discussion Note, September 7.

Parker, J. (2009). World Bank Chief Paul Wolfowitz Resigns. *ABC News*. At https://abcnews.go.com/ Politics/story?id=3152373&page=1.

Patel, K. K. (2016). *The New Deal: A Global History*. Princeton: Princeton University Press.

Polanyi, K. (1944). *The Great Transformation: The Political and Economic Origins of Our Time*. New York: Farrar and Rinehart.

Pollin, R. (2020). An Industrial Policy Framework to Advance a Global Green New Deal. In A. Oqubay et al. (eds.), *The Oxford Handbook of Industrial Policy*. Oxford: Oxford University Press.

Poon, D. and R. Kozul-Wright (2019). Catch-Up and the Making of China's Developmental State. In A. Oqubay and K. Ohno (eds.), *How Nations Learn: Technological Learning, Industrial Policy and Catch-Up.* Oxford: Oxford University Press.

Prasad, E. (2015). *The Dollar Trap.* Oxford: Oxford University Press.

Prasad, E. (2016). *Gaining Currency: The Rise of the Renminbi.* Oxford: Oxford University Press.

Rauchway, E. (2018). *Winter War: Hoover, Roosevelt, and the First Clash over the New Deal.* New York: Basic Books.

Rodrik, D. (2006). The Social Cost of Foreign Exchange Reserves. *International Economic Journal* 20(3), 253–66.

Rodrik, D. (2011). *The Globalization Paradox: Democracy and the Future of the World Economy.* New York: W. W. Norton.

Rodrik, D. (2015). Premature Deindustrialization. *Journal of Economic Growth* 21, 1–33.

Rogoff, K. (2019). The Case for a World Carbon Bank. *Project Syndicate*, July 8. At https://www.project-syndicate.org/commentary/world-carbon-bank-for-developing-countries-by-kenneth-rogoff-2019-07.

Sachs, L. and L. Johnson (2019). Investment Treaties, Investor–State Dispute Settlement and Inequality: How International Rules and Institutions Can Exacerbate Domestic Disparities. *SSRN*. At http://dx.doi.org/10.2139/ssrn.3452136.

Schlesinger, A. (1958). *The Age of Roosevelt: The*

Coming of the New Deal. Boston: Houghton Mifflin Company.

Shadlen, K. C. (2005). Exchanging Development for Market Access? Deep Integration and Industrial Policy under Multilateral and Regional-Bilateral Trade Agreements. *Review of International Political Economy* 12(5), 750–75.

Shapiro, J. (2021). The Environmental Bias of Trade Policy. *Quarterly Journal of Economics* 36(2), 831–86.

Shaxson, N. (2018). *The Finance Curse: How Global Finance Is Making Us All Poorer*. London: Bodley Head.

Skidelsky, R. (2000). *John Maynard Keynes: Fighting for Freedom, 1937–1946*. New York: Viking.

Stiglitz, J. et al. (2010). *The Stiglitz Report: Reforming the International and Monetary and Financial Systems in the Wake of Global Crises*. New York: The New Press.

Studart, R. and K. Gallagher (2018). Guaranteeing Sustainable Infrastructure. *International Economics* 155(C), 84–91.

Swedberg, R. (1986). The Doctrine of Economic Neutrality of the IMF and the World Bank. *Journal of Peace Research* 23(4), 377–90.

Temin, P. (2010). The Great Recession and the Great Depression. NBER Working Paper no. 15645.

Temin, P. and D. Vines (2013). *The Leaderless Economy:*

Bibliography

Why the World Economy Fell Apart and How to Fix it. Princeton: Princeton University Press.

Thrasher, R. and K. P. Gallagher (2020). Domestic Resource Mobilization and the Trade and Investment Regime. Global Development Policy Center, Boston University.

Tienhaara, K. and Cotula, L. (2020). *Raising the Cost of Climate Action? Investor–State Dispute Settlement and Compensation for Stranded Fossil Fuel Assets*. London: IIED.

Tooze, A. (2014). *The Deluge: The Great War and the Making of Global Order, 1916–1931*. London: Allen Lane.

Tooze, A. (2019). Everything You Know about Global Order Is Wrong. *Foreign Affairs*, January 30.

UNCTAD (various years). Trade and Development Report, Geneva United Nations Conference on Trade and Development.

United Nations General Assembly (UNGA) (2015). Basic Principles on Sovereign Debt Restructuring Processes. At https://unctad.org/system/files/official-document/a69L84_en.pdf.

US Secretary of the Treasury (1959). Final Report on the Reconstruction Finance Corporation. US Government Printing Office, Washington, DC.

Varoufakis, Y. (2013). *The Global Minotaur: America, Europe and the Future of the Global Economy*. London: Zed.

Volz, U. and S. J. Ahmed (2020). *Macrofinancial Risks in Climate Vulnerable Developing Countries and the Role of the IMF: Towards a Joint V20–IMF Action Agenda*. London, Rotterdam, and Bonn: SOAS Centre for Sustainable Finance, Global Center on Adaptation, and Munich Climate Insurance Initiative.

Winkler, H., S. Keen, and A. Marquard (2020). *Climate Finance to Transform Energy Infrastructure as Part of a Just Transition in South Africa*. Research Report for SNAPFI project, University of Cape Town.

World Bank (2018). Press Release: World Bank Group Shareholders Endorse Transformative Capital Package. April 21. At http://www.worldbank.org/en/news/press-release/2018/04/21/world-bank-group-shareholders-endorse-transformative-capital-package.

World Bank (2019). Global Infrastructure Facility. At https://www.globalinfrafacility.org/sites/gif/files/GIF_Overview.pdf.

World Bank (2020). Private Participation in Infrastructure Annual Report. At https://ppi.worldbank.org/en/ppi.

World Inequality (2020). World Inequality Database. At www.wid.world.

WTO (2020). Regional Trade Agreements. At https://www.wto.org/english/tratop_e/region_e/region_e.htm.

WTO-UNEP (2009). Trade and Climate Change. At http://tinyurl.com/WTO-UNEP.

Xu J., R. Marodon, and X. Ru (2020). Identifying and Classifying Public Development Banks and

Development Finance Institutions. Research Paper no. 192, AFD, Paris. At https://www.afd.fr/sites/afd/files/2020–11–12–01–08/PR192VA_Identify_Classify_PDBs_DFIs.pdf.